RELENTLESS PURSUIT

RELENTLESS PURSUIT

PETA TABERNER

Hope Ministries International

Contents

Printed by IngramSpark
ISBN: 978-0-9756199-0-2
ISBN eBook: 978-0-9756199-1-9

First Printing, 2024

ACKNOWLEDGEMENTS

Firstly, my biggest thanks goes to my King, my Saviour, the One I adore above all others, the One whom my soul loves, my Friend and my Lord, Jesus Christ. Thank you for Your Relentless Pursuit of me.

A massive thank you to my incredible husband, Lee. You are my best friend, my love, my rock. I wouldn't want to be walking this journey with anyone else. Also, to our amazing children and gorgeous grand-children, apart from Jesus, you are my greatest treasures. I love you all beyond measure.

To my beautiful Mum, thank you so very much. Without your constant prayers I know I wouldn't be where I am today. I love you millions.

To my Dad (in heaven), thank you for being such a wonderful ex-ample of what a Father should be. You made it so easy for me to know my Heavenly Father. Keep cheering, I'll see you again soon!!

Thank you to my amazing friends and senior leaders, Daniel and Chelsea Hagen. It is an honour and privilege to serve the Lord alongside you both - you are champions for the Kingdom and Heaven celebrates you. Lee and I love and appreciate you so much.

To Anton and Bev Bekker, thank you for your love and support, for challenging me and encouraging me. Thank you, Bev for all your work in editing this book, I couldn't have done it without you.

ENDORSEMENTS

I was so honoured when Peta asked me to write an endorsement for her book, *Relentless Pursuit*. She is a great friend with a wealth of spirit-filled knowledge, and I was excited to read it. And I wasn't disappointed! This is such an engaging read for both Christians and non-Christians. It will fuel the fire of any Christian reader and fill the heart of every reader with the knowledge of God's love and plan for us all.

From the early days of a life away from God, hurt by the church, walking in sin, to a true, life changing salvation, this story will keep you reading from beginning to end! Peta has created a fantastic evangelism tool with a very real, raw story. I know Peta and Lee personally and would class them as two of the closest friends I have on Planet Earth.

Seeing their lives lived out for Jesus is such a challenge and inspiration to me and my wife Breezy. Peta and Lee, Hope Ministries International, keep doing what you're doing, making Jesus famous! This book is a testament to the grace and anointing that is on your life.

Daz Chettle, Director of Harvest Now School of Evangelism

"In Psalm 63:8 David declares the passion of his soul in desperate pursuit of God and His presence. In the years that I have known Peta and Lee Taberner, this kind, humble and powerful couple always reveal a deep craving for more and more of the supernatural reality of God. *Relentless Pursuit* is raw and honest and reveals, not just God's pursuit of two young people lost and drowning in a drug-soaked world, but reveals their pursuit of King Jesus after He revealed Himself so powerfully to them.

As you read their story you will be encouraged and challenged to pursue God, knowing that if He could pick Peta and Lee out of the Devil's grasp, transforming them into powerful, impacting servants of the Lord, He can do amazing things with your life.

It has been a wonderful privilege to know them and work with them on a number of occasions.

Evangelist Tim Hall, Tim Hall Ministries International

Romans 10:13-15 TPT proclaims, *"Everyone who calls on the name of the Lord will be rescued and experience new life. But how can people call on Him for help if they've not yet believed? And how can they believe in one they've not yet heard of? And how can they hear the message of life if there is no one there to proclaim it? And how can the message be proclaimed if messengers have yet to be sent? That's why the Scriptures say: "How welcome is the arrival of those proclaiming the joyful news of peace and of good things to come!"*

There is nothing more fulfilling in life than to witness lives that are transformed in the purest way, through an encounter with the power of the unconditional love of God. Deep within us all, as ones created by a living God, is a longing for 'home' a need for belonging, a need to be loved, a need to be seen and a cry to be identified.

His beloved children Peta and Lee, who have been profoundly found and transformed by God, have sold their lives out with a passion of *Relentless Pursuit* to seek out those who, like themselves, have come to the end of the road and desperately need the message of life.

We have witnessed with our own eyes the radical transformation of Peta and Lee's lives and the impact they have made on so many lives in return through Hope Ministries International.

We are proud to call them our spiritual son and daughter.

For those of you who are searching, may this book of memoirs enlighten you to a God who is calling you by name and for those of you who know Him, may it light a passion in you to awaken to the cry of the lost.

Pastors Phil and Julie Oldfield, C3 Church Tuggerah, New South Wales, Australia

In *Relentless Pursuit*, my dear friend Peta masterfully unveils the captivating story of God's unyielding pursuit of His children. With vulnerabilities and depth, the book reveals the ceaseless love that transcends every boundary. It's a profound exploration of faith, reminding us that God's relentless pursuit is an unwavering beacon of hope. This compelling read invites readers to embark on a spiritual journey that will leave hearts stirred and souls uplifted - a testament to the enduring connection between God and His beloved children."

Evangelist Andrew Cannon, Founder of Gospel Grenades. Author of *Dare To Share*.

Peta Taberner is one of the most on-fire women of God I have ever met. I am so thankful for the way she and her family, especially her husband Lee, continue to pursue God, and for the consistent character they have displayed over many years. It's such a blessing to many that she has now written this book, as it details the profound way God met them whilst in a very dark place of sin and dependency in their own personal lives. She shares very vulnerably how Jesus transformed them and has given us all keys and tools to prepare us for the mission field. As they have trusted in the divine power of God's hand on their lives, this book will leave you refreshed and encouraged by the testimonies of powerful stories of God's intervention. You will be equipped and reminded that there is no one God cannot use and that no one is so far away from Him that He cannot save them. I fully support her and am so thankful for Peta and her heart to share *Relentless Pursuit* with us! Read it with faith and expectation, as I believe the Lord will jump off the pages and ignite fire in your heart.

Ben Fitzgerald, Senior Leader - Awakening Europe

As you read *Relentless Pursuit*, you will be taken on a riveting journey, a testimony of Gods faithfulness. You will laugh, cry and be inspired to relentlessly pursue God. Peta and Lee's journey is full of inspiring stories that will leave you encouraged. I highly recommend this book for everyone.

Pastor James NJino, Victory Life Church Towoomba, Queensland, Australia

This book is dedicated to each and every person
who recognises the Relentless Pursuit of God in their own
life, and encounters His love through the pages of this book.

FOREWORD

In 2017, Daniel and I had the pleasure of meeting Peta and Lee Taberner.

We were fortunate to join them in revival outreach tent meetings in Orange, New South Wales, where we were deeply moved as we witnessed numerous signs, wonders, and miracles, along with powerful altar calls where people were saved, healed, delivered and baptised. We felt a very strong Kingdom connection straight away, which has continued to this day.

Peta and Lee's passion and zeal for winning the lost is truly inspiring. Their impactful work in Australia and abroad includes expanding God's Kingdom through weekly feeding programs for the homeless, collaborating with First Nation communities, organising revival tent meetings, and empowering the body of Christ through training and activating evangelism ministry schools. Thanks to their efforts, countless individuals have experienced the saving grace of the Lord Jesus Christ through Hope Ministries International.

Their unwavering commitment to the Gospel is truly inspiring. They fearlessly dedicate themselves to Jesus, regardless of the circumstances. Their steadfastness and determination to press forward without looking back is admirable.

We fully endorse *Relentless Pursuit*. It is both impacting and influential, whether you are standing at a crossroads or seeking to deepen your understanding of God's love. God has beautifully woven an incredible tapestry through this powerful couple's lives; a raw, poignant story from destruction and despair to victorious redemption and restoration.

What I love most about this book is how Peta's story demonstrates that, regardless of where we find ourselves in this life, God is in hot pursuit of our hearts. He is not willing that any should perish. I love the risk of faith - denying themselves and stepping out for God when it makes no sense to leave a world of privilege and luxury; leaving it all behind for Jesus Christ to hit the road to see revival.

Peta Taberner doesn't simply write about Jesus Christ; she embodies the Gospel message through her lived example of faithfulness, integrity, and honesty. The true impact of this book lies in its ability to spark change within the reader. You cannot simply walk away unaffected. Not only will you know the relentless, pursuing love, grace and extreme goodness of God, but as you close this book, there will be an echoing victory, your spirit charged to seek relentlessly after God. It ignites a desire to lay down more for the Gospel, compels a commitment to serving as His hands and feet, and leaves you brimming with fresh inspiration to impact the world around you.

With heartfelt recommendation,

Daniel and Chelsea Hagen, Overseers Fire Church Ministries

INTRODUCTION

We often say, or hear it said, how we "found God", but is that really accurate? Was He ever hidden from us? Were we even looking for Him? Or was it He who was pursuing us all along?

From the beginning, starting with the book of Genesis in the Bible, God creates human beings for relationship with Himself. After Adam and Eve eat the fruit and realise they are naked, they hide themselves from God and it is God Himself who pursues them, *"Then the Lord God called to Adam and said to him, "Where are you?""* (Genesis 3:9)

The Parable of the Lost Sheep gives an intimate view of the God who pursues us:

"What man of you, having a hundred sheep, if he loses one of them, does not leave the ninety-nine in the wilderness, and go after the one which is lost until he finds it? And when he has found it, he lays it on his shoulders, rejoicing. And when he comes home, he calls together his friends and neighbours, saying to them, 'Rejoice with me, for I have found my sheep which was lost!'" (Luke 15:4-6 NKJV).

Evangelist Daniel Kolenda puts it this way:

> *One of the major differences between Christianity and all the other religions of the world is that in every other religion it is man seeking god (or gods), but in Christianity it is God seeking man. In Christianity, all of the intention, all of the initiative is on the part of God. If He had not initiated the rescue mission to save us, we would have no chance, no hope. He is the One who was looking for us!*

The entire Bible is the story of God's passionate pursuit of us - the Creator seeking out His lost creation. His heart has always been for the reconciliation between us and Himself, even when we aren't looking for Him.

"The Lord says, "I was ready to respond, but no one asked for help. I was ready to be found, but no one was looking for me. I said, 'Here I am, here I am!' to a nation that did not call on my name. All day long I opened my arms to a rebellious people. But they follow their own evil paths and their own crooked schemes." (Isaiah 65:1-2 NLT)

God's relentless pursuit of us involved sending His beloved Son to earth, to walk among the people He loved and to then die in their place. Because there was absolutely nothing that we could do to bridge the gap that sin had created between us and Him, God reached out to us. The Bible says, "for the Son of Man has come to seek and to save that which was lost." (Luke 19:10 AMP)

He continues to reach out to us today. He continues to relentlessly pursue us. His is a love that's willing to go to the ends of the earth to reach us.

"Where can I go from Your Spirit? Or where can I flee from Your presence? If I ascend into heaven, You are there; If I make my bed in hell, behold, You are there." (Psalm 139:7-8)

When I started writing this book, I had no idea what the title would be, until I started seeing how God had actively and relentlessly pursued both Lee and I throughout our lives. Now that we are looking back, His love, grace and mercy is so very evident. Tears of gratitude ran down my face many times whilst writing, as I saw how His hand was on us and His presence surrounded us even in our darkest days. I am so thankful for His protection that surrounded us while we were walking so far away from Him.

"Surely Your goodness and unfailing love will pursue me all the days of my life..." (Psalm 23:6)

This verse is so true for us. We were found by a God we weren't even looking for and we are forever grateful to Him.

If you're a Christian reading this book, I pray that you will take the time to look back on your own journey and see the relentless pursuit of God for you. Remember the ways He protected you, remember the way He drew you by His Spirit, remember the moment He captured your heart and that first love you had for Him.

If you don't yet know God, my prayer is that as you read through these pages, you will open your heart to Him, and ask Him to reveal Himself to you, and that you will see that He has been relentlessly pursuing you. I pray that you will encounter Him personally and experience the unconditional and unfailing love that He has just for you.

I

EARLY YEARS

LEE

Lee was born in November 1967 in Orange, New South Wales. He was the fourth son of five boys born to Graham and Lois Taberner. Lee's parents were childhood sweethearts and although they have both passed away now, Lois and Graham both shared stories of their younger days with me.

Lois and Graham grew up in a very strict religion (more like a cult) and were kicked out of home at a young age when they were caught sleeping together. They were left to fend for themselves, as a result of which Lee's father turned to crime and ended up spending a short time in prison. Lois had no way of supporting herself and so returned to live with her parents (who were still in the religion). She was locked in a caravan, told to read the Bible and was only allowed out to attend church. At what would be the last service she attended, the minister spoke from the pulpit and said, "There is someone in here who shouldn't be here" and pointed straight at Lois. Lois, feeling so humiliated, got up, walked out of the church, and never returned.

Ostracised by their families because of the religion, Lee's parents brought their boys up very differently; the boys grew up with the perception that religion (or anything associated with God) was bad, because of the misrepresentation of God their parents had experienced.

However, God says in the Bible (Isaiah 55:11) that His words will not return to Him void, so the small seeds that were planted in Lee's parent's hearts and minds from the Word of God were remembered. They taught their boys when they were young to pray before bedtime and although Lois and Graham didn't attend church again, the knowledge that there was a God remained.

Lee's parents did their absolute best to raise their boys well and they all grew up to be amazing men. Unfortunately, however, alcohol played a very big part in their lives and as a result of that upbringing Lee made a lot of wrong choices in his life. He was just fourteen years old when he was given a bag of marijuana which started him on a downward spiral into a world of drugs and crime, where he would remain for the next 12 years. By the age of nineteen, Lee was not only drinking heavily and using drugs, but also selling drugs to support his habit.

PETA

I was born in September 1972, in Gosford on the Central Coast of NSW to Peter and Ann Hulbert. I was the middle child of three girls, each born about seven years apart.

My upbringing was a very happy one. Mum stayed home with us while Dad worked away quite a bit. The family would often join him in different areas of the country for holidays. I was very close to my dad, often telling my sisters that I was the favourite.

Our family lived on the Central Coast until 1983, when Mum and Dad decided to move so that Dad could have a more central base for work. They found a property in Mudgee, New South Wales, on which they signed contract, but it fell through just before settlement. Disappointed, they were driving back to the Central Coast when they decided to take a detour and drive through Orange. While there, they stopped in at a local real estate and found a block of land which they fell in love with and bought straightaway. Within a few months we had moved to Orange and lived in a caravan on the land while Mum and Dad built their dream home.

The fact that we ended up in Orange (not Mudgee), was such a God-ordered step on our journey. If we had not moved to Orange, this story could have been very different.

Although we never attended church (except for christenings and the like), Mum had a knowledge of God from her childhood.

NAN MARY

In 1980 my grandmother (Mum's mum), moved to Australia from England. Not long after she arrived, we found out she had terminal cancer. By the time we moved to Orange in 1983, she was quite unwell. Nan wasn't a Christian, but she asked my mum to find a minister who believed in healing to come and lay hands on her and pray. Mum had absolutely no idea what she meant.

At that moment, just after that very conversation, there was a knock at the door which Mum went to answer. There was a lady standing at the door who we didn't know. She said, "I saw you had Shetland puppies for sale". (Mum was breeding dogs at the time but you couldn't see the puppies from the road, nor were they for sale).

Mum replied, "No, we don't". Then Nan called out to Mum from the bedroom. The lady noticed Mum was worried and asked if every-thing was okay and if there was anything she could do, to which Mum replied, "You don't know anyone who believes in healing do you?"

The lady replied, "As a matter of fact I do; if I can I use your phone, I'll call my pastor right now". She called and the pastor arrived within fifteen minutes!

When he arrived, he spent time talking with Nan and prayed with her. That day Nan gave her life to Jesus and then insisted we all attend this pastor's church.

Nan ended up in hospital not long after this, but she was allowed out to attend church and so we continued to go. People from the church helped Mum get Nan to and from the church and the pastor and others from the church came to visit her every day. They also made meals for our family and looked after me and my sister as Mum was at the hospital a lot of the time, and Dad was up in the Northern Territory (Darwin) working. The church became like our family. At some point during this time Mum and I said a prayer of salvation with the pastor in Nan's hospital room, but we didn't really understand exactly what it meant.

Unfortunately, Nan didn't receive her physical healing here on earth and she passed away on the 8th of March, 1984.

Her dying wish was that Mum would keep attending that church and continue to take me and my sisters to church there.

JESUS IN THE BACKYARD

During the same year that I gave my heart to Jesus for the first time, Lee also had an encounter with Him!

Lee, who was seventeen in 1984, was already heavily addicted to drugs. He was having suicidal thoughts and thought he was going crazy. He was working full time at Grace Bro's (now called Myer) in Orange, and once a week after work he would secretly drive to Sydney (a three-hour drive away) to see a psychiatrist.

One night, after returning home, he walked in the back door of his family home and glanced out the kitchen window (which overlooked the neighbour's property). He saw Jesus standing in the neighbour's backyard. Thinking he was seeing things, he looked away quickly and walked into the lounge room, but couldn't resist having another look! He peered around the corner, back out the kitchen window, and there was Jesus still standing there looking back at him. This continued for around thirty minutes; Lee would walk away but felt drawn to look again. Jesus never left; he was still standing in the same place looking back until Lee finally went to bed.

Remembering this event recently, Lee remarked, "I wish I could say I immediately gave up alcohol and drugs and started following Christ, but unfortunately that didn't happen. However, from that day on I never had another suicidal thought and had no need to return to the psychiatrist!"

EARLY CHURCH DAYS

After Nan Mary passed away my mum, my younger sister and I started attending church quite regularly. It wasn't too long before I started to understand salvation and consequently responded to an altar call one evening. I made a public decision to give my life to Jesus at the age of twelve.

We all became very involved in church life and found ourselves at church or various church meetings more often than we were at home. Whether is was prayer meetings, midweek meetings, youth group, two Sunday services or whatever else was on - we were there! After about a year my father also made a commitment to follow Christ and began attending church with us.

For the next couple of years, I was totally committed to the church and loved Jesus with all my heart. At the time I played the guitar and joined the worship team. I would spend hours in my room with the Lord, worshiping and reading the Bible. My Bible from those early years is so well used, it is barely held together.

I remember my mum walked into my bedroom one afternoon as I was worshipping. She stopped suddenly near the door and (seeing in the Spirit), said, "Wow, there are angels all around the room!"

It was during this time, in my early teen years, that I received very specific prophetic words about future ministry and seeing thousands saved. There was nothing I wanted more.

Each week we would go down the Main Street in Orange, New South Wales. Mum would stand on the post office steps with her guitar, singing to the Lord, and other team members would share the Gospel with passers-by.

An older man who we didn't know would also preach nearby in a laneway, called Post Office Lane. He would preach on hell, fire and brimstone with such passion, warning people, pleading with them, to repent! Years later I found out that this was Lee's grandfather. Lee would often have been sitting nearby, listening to his grandfather, as seeds of the Gospel were planted in his life.

I have learnt an important lesson from this part of our story. The Bible talks about seed time and harvest, about the importance of sowing seeds. (Genesis 8:22)

I often used to think that successful evangelism comes down to how many decisions are made for Christ. However, if no seeds are sown first, there can be no harvest! I have come to understand that successful evangelism is simply about obedience - am I obedient to share the gospel, to plant a seed or water the seed someone else planted? I am not responsible for the decisions others make; I am only accountable for myself.

I am also encouraged to remember that it is God who brings the increase (success). The Bible says in 1 Corinthians 3 that one person sows, another waters, but it is God who brings the increase. We also have the assurance that God's word will not return to Him void, *"So shall My word be that goes forth from My mouth; It shall not return to Me void, but it shall accomplish what I please, and it shall prosper in the thing for which I sent it."* (Isaiah 55:11)

God is wanting so much more than our talents or abilities; He wants us to surrender our talents to Him, to be available with a 'Yes Lord', and to simply obey Him.

ENCOUNTERING THE HOLY SPIRIT

1985.

The Holy Spirit is such a beautiful and powerful part of who God is and such an essential part of our Christian walk. It is the Holy Spirit who first draws us to the Father, and it is He who first convicts us of sin. Once we are living as a believer, He is there to guide us, to comfort and to teach us, to counsel us, to help us and correct us, to empower us and to intercede for us. We need the Holy Spirit in every area of our lives. After Mum and I had been attending the church for little while and we had given our lives to Jesus and been water baptised, we still weren't sure about the Holy Spirit (and in particular about the manifestations of the Spirit, for e.g., falling over or being 'slain in the Spirit').

One night, we had a visiting preacher at the church. I have to laugh as I remember how Mum and I had decided that we would both go for prayer and if he could make us fall over without touching us, then we would believe!

So, the visiting preacher preached, and I have no idea what he preached on. Then he called people forward to the altar if they wanted a touch from the Holy Spirit. Mum and I looked at each other and said, "well, here we go!"

The altar was packed, and we ended up in a big, long line, separated from each other. The preacher started praying at one end of the line, telling us to close our eyes and lift our hands. I don't think Mum and I did either of those things because Mum was watching me to see if anything was going to happen. Next thing I know, people started falling all around me and I literally felt a force push me backwards onto the ground; my eyes were open and there was no one near me at all (except someone behind me to catch me, thankfully!).

As my mum was watching this happen the exact same thing happened to her - again with no one around her. We both lay there on the floor in shock; neither of us could get up for quite some time. Later that night when it was time to leave, Mum was still so affected by the power of God that she was unable to drive home!

Needless to say, we never doubted the power of the Holy Spirit after that night. We had experienced for ourselves what the Bible teaches in Acts 2! The Holy Spirit empowers us to be witnesses for the Gospel, gives us supernatural gifts, and anoints us to fulfil our purpose. Jesus knows we need the Holy Spirit. He says in John 16:7, *"Nevertheless I tell you the truth. It is to your advantage that I go away; for if I do not go away, the Helper will not come to you; but if I depart, I will send Him to you."*

It is not possible for me to live the way I am called to live without the Holy Spirit. He is so necessary to us every single day. He leads us into all truth (John 16:13), He directs our steps (Romans 8:9). He gives us boldness (Acts 2). He is our seal and guarantee (Ephesians 1:13-14). He is our source of revelation and wisdom (1 Corinthians 2:10-11). He intercedes for us (Romans 8:26-27). He sanctifies us (Romans 15:16) and He is our advocate (John 14:26).

In Acts 2, after Jesus had ascended to Heaven, the promised Holy Spirit was poured out on the hundred or so people gathered together in the upper room. Immediately, they began to speak in tongues, they were filled with boldness, and they began to preach!

People were amazed at the outpouring - there were signs and wonders as the crowd of many different nations each heard the disciples speaking in their own language. As Peter preached, the crowd was convicted and many repented and were saved. The Holy Spirit's work had begun, and continues to this day to fill us, to give us gifts, to fill us with boldness, to demonstrate the power of God, and to convict us of sin. The precious Holy Spirit - the manifest power of God, is vital for us to know Him, to learn how to relate to Him and to understand how He manifests (clearly reveals) Himself.

HURTS AND DISAPPOINTMENTS

1987.

As time went by, Mum became involved in various areas of ministry in the church, and we became very close to quite a few families who made up the leadership team. However, the more involved Mum became, the more she realised some things weren't quite right. A few years down the track, in 1987, 80% of the leadership including the senior pastor, abruptly left and the church suffered a major split. To me, not knowing exactly what had happened or why, it was like my family was being torn apart. We had spent the last few years doing life together, growing together, worshipping together. Now we were separated, and I was devastated!

At about the same time, I was becoming a little rebellious (my mum would probably say more than a little!). After just a couple of weeks into Year Nine, I left school. I didn't see the need for schooling as I had no desire for a career and didn't enjoy studying anything. I was feeling very uncertain after the church split and I no longer wanted to attend church. But I did stay in close contact with some of the leaders. To protect innocent families, I won't go into too much detail, except to say that the people who I had looked up to as leaders were definitely not walking as they should have been.

It didn't take long for me to start drifting away from God as I saw Him being misrepresented by those who should have been leading and protecting us. I had begun drinking and smoking cigarettes and one night I, along with another young girlfriend from church, was drinking with one of these leaders. He was a married man with children. Much later that night, for reasons I cannot even remember, we decided to go for a drive. I was fourteen and had way too much to drink, but jumped in the car with this man anyway. We ended up in a park where things happened that shouldn't have, and following that night, continued to happen for quite a while afterwards.

I was hurt, disillusioned, angry and disappointed. I felt such brokenness, but instead of reaching out to the only One who could heal me, I went looking elsewhere. Being so young and vulnerable, I made a number of wrong decisions around this time and started hanging out with the wrong crowd. I ended up walking away from the church altogether and started my journey down a pretty dark path, wanting nothing more to do with God. For me, God was now tarnished by the way His people had misrepresented Him.

Although I walked as far away from God as I could, He continually pursued me; His love was always reaching out to me, His eyes stayed upon me, His hand always protecting me. Looking back now from a place of leadership and having seen and experienced first-hand the damage that is caused when God is misrepresented, both Lee and I are so conscious of our walk with God and how we represent Him. The world is always watching, the church is always watching and our children are always watching. If we aren't living what we're preaching, then there's something wrong. If our children and families are seeing someone different at home compared to what others are seeing when we preach or as we minister, then there's something wrong.

I'm definitely not saying we are perfect! Of course, we all make mistakes, but we are always mindful that we need to be pursuing holiness. As the Bible encourages us, *"But just as He who called you is holy, so be holy in all you do; for it is written: "Be holy, because I am holy."* (1 Peter 1:15-16)

We may have an amazing gift or calling on our life, but without the integrity and character to carry that gift, so much damage can be done. Godly character will sustain us wherever our gifts take us!

The Bible says in Romans 11:29, *"For the gifts and the calling of God are irrevocable."* (Some versions say 'with-out repentance'). We can all operate in the gifts God gives us, but if we continue to operate in the gifts, but live a compromised life (when what we preach and believe doesn't match what we do), we are walking a very dangerous road.

In Matthew it says, *"Many will say to Me in that day, 'Lord, Lord, have we not prophesied in Your name, cast out demons in Your name, and done many wonders in Your name?' And then I will declare to them, 'I never knew you; depart from Me, you who practice lawlessness!'"*

This verse keeps me pursuing a close relationship with Jesus. It is talking about the fact that I can be operating in the gifts of the Spirit, perhaps be in ministry, praying and prophesying, casting out demons and healing the sick in the name of Jesus, moving in the power of God, and yet living in continual, unrepentant sin, living without KNOWING Him intimately or having Him KNOW me.

Unless I am in relationship with Him, surrendered to Him in that intimate place of holy friendship so that I am able to bear fruit that lasts, walking in integrity and allowing Him to build my character so that it mirrors His, I not only risk hearing the words 'depart from me', I also risk turning others away when they see the hypocrisy, the lies and the sin (it will be exposed sooner or later, guaranteed).

2

THE BEGINNING OF OUR
JOURNEY TOGETHER

DRUG DELIVERY

A ugust 1988.
Once I'd made the decision to walk away from God, it didn't take long to get caught up in the world of drugs, alcohol and whatever went along with it. One evening, in August 1988, I was at a friend's house getting ready to go to the pub (yes, underage!) for our usual week-end partying. Before we left, we had organised to get some marijuana delivered. I was sitting on my friend's lounge room floor, waiting, when there was a knock at the door and in walked Lee (the dealer home delivered!). I think we both did a double take thinking he/she looks okay, but neither of us said anything to each other. He dropped off the marijuana, my girlfriend and I smoked it, and we went out for the night.

Lee had asked my friend where I lived, so the next day he came and knocked on the front door. My mum answered the door as I was in bed nursing a hangover. When I finally got to the door, Lee asked if I'd like to go out with him that night. My head was pounding, and I said no, shut the door, turned around and went back to bed. The very next day, however, I found out where he lived, went to visit him, and never left!

I pretty much moved in with him that afternoon. I was just two weeks away from my sixteenth birthday and Lee was twenty-one. My parents were definitely not impressed!

The house we were living in was like a drug den; there was another guy living there and countless people coming and going at all times of the day or night. Both Lee and I have such vague memories of living there. We were very rarely not either high or drunk. After a couple of months of living there, we all had to move out rather quickly and Lee and I moved back in with our parents for a short time.

By early the following year we had found another house, moved in and our journey together began.

STILL, SMALL VOICE

December 1988.

Even though I was living a life that was in direct opposition to what I knew God wanted and I had no desire to follow Him or have anything to do with His people, deep down there was always that still small voice trying to draw me back to Himself. And there was always my mum praying for us!

Never underestimate the power of a praying Mum!

Philippians 1:6 says, *"being confident of this very thing, that He who has begun a good work in you will complete it until the day of Jesus Christ;"*

The Lord promises over and over again in the Bible that He will never leave us or forsake us. I love what He says to Jacob in Genesis 28:15, *"Behold, I am with you and will keep you wherever you go and will bring you back to this land; for I will not leave you until I have done what I have spoken to you."* The same is true for us today; even when we are faithless, He remains faithful. (2 Timothy 2:13).

One thing I remember from those early days was a little nativity scene I had. There were separate pieces - Mary, Joseph, little lambs, shepherds, and baby Jesus. I would keep these nativity pieces set up all year round on the record player in our house. Every afternoon Lee would flip open the top of the record player to play music and the little pieces would go flying. When he was done, I would set them all back up again. I also kept my Bible. I still have it to this day and as I mentioned previously, it is barely held together. I would often pull it out when no one was around and stare at the life-giving words in that book. Then I would remember that His people were a joke - they talked the talk, but didn't walk the walk.

> *The greatest single cause of atheism in the world today is Christians who acknowledge Jesus with their lips, walk out the door, and deny Him by their lifestyle. That is what an unbelieving world simply finds unbelievable.*
> Brennan Manning

Matthew 15:8 says, *"These people draw near to Me with their mouth, and honour Me with their lips, but their heart is far from Me."* I think many of us have, sadly, encountered those who misrepresent God. People who for one reason or another call themselves "Christians", but live in total opposition to what the word represents, not reflecting the true nature and character of God.

And so, for the first few years of our journey together, our lives simply revolved around drugs, alcohol, and partying. All our friends were the same. Most of them are not alive today as a direct result of this lifestyle. Looking back, it's hard to understand how we thought this was living, but we did, just as many others do today. We were caught in a world that had nothing more to offer. We were searching for truth, searching for love, searching for fulfilment, searching for success, trying to cover the pain, hurt and disappointment in our lives, not knowing that it could only be found in the One who created us.

LOAN DENIED

1989.

About a year or so into our relationship, we were living a pretty compromised lifestyle. We were heavily addicted to drugs, as well as selling them and involved in different types of criminal activity.

One evening, having no money whatsoever, I worked up the courage to go and ask for help. I knocked on the door of a pastor's house that I knew in Orange. I must've looked pretty bad and was reluctantly invited inside. I asked the pastor for a loan of $10 to buy bread and milk; his reply was, "I would have to ask the board" (meaning the church board of elders).

I told him not to worry about it and abruptly left. Determined to avenge this denial of finances, Lee jumped the back fence into the pastor's yard and stole his lawnmower. Although not the best response, this was, however, better than doing over the church for the offerings, which was another idea that we had, but thankfully never followed through.

The pastor's response to my request was another misrepresentation of who God is and how He yearns for us to know Him. It was another reason for me to justify walking away from the church and I hardened my heart towards God even more.

The Bible says, "...*the goodness of God leads man to repentance.*" (Romans 2:4), and "*while we were still sinners, Christ died for us.*" (Romans 5:8). Regardless of how close, or how far, someone is from Christ, it is so important to not be judgemental of the situations or lifestyles that people are in, but to show His love, to let His compassion and His heart for them flow out of us. We don't know what led someone to be in the situation they are in, what led them to alcohol or drugs, or what has caused them to be homeless, and we don't know what hurt they are carrying. When the woman who was found in adultery was brought before Jesus, He didn't condemn her but showed grace and mercy towards her (John 8). The only One who was qualified to throw a stone at her, didn't.

Am I saying that pastor should've given me money at that time? No, not at all; Lee and I now run homeless programs and rarely give out money to homeless, drunk or drug affected people. But an offer of bread and milk would've gone a long way. Our teams are regularly out on the streets amongst the homeless, those who are on all sorts of drugs, and the alcoholics. We run feeding programs and organise sleeping bags and toiletries, we've given out thousands of food hampers over the years, and we make sure that every single person who receives from us or our team hears the gospel and feels seen, heard and loved.

As a Christian, I may be the only form of Jesus that some people will ever see. We are Jesus' hands and feet. I am absolutely convicted of this and cannot emphasise the point enough - we must represent Him well!

CAR ACCIDENT

October 1991.

By 1991, my parents had moved to the Central Coast while Lee and I still lived in Orange. On a weekend visit to the Central Coast, when I was around six months pregnant with our first child, we went to a car auction in Newcastle to purchase a new car. It needed some work done on it and wasn't ready to be driven all the way back home, so Lee caught a train home to return to work and I stayed with my parents for a few days until it was ready.

On the day I picked up the car I went straight to a local dealer to get some drugs for the drive home. Apart from this day, I can't remember a time when I wasn't under the influence of drugs while driving. On this day, however, I wasn't able to get any drugs before I left, so I started out on the four-hour drive home, straight and sober.

While driving through the Blue Mountains, I drove through an oil spill on the road and lost control of the car. The car spun a few times, hitting the guardrail (praise God there was a guardrail, saving us from a certain death rolling down the mountain), then ended up wedging itself against a cliff-face. The car was written off and virtually undrive-able, but apart from a bump on the head and being very shaken, I, and the baby I was carrying, was absolutely fine. God continually shows His faithfulness and mercy - His protection over our lives was undeniable.

This accident really started me thinking again about the life I was living. Deep down I knew the truth - I felt that if I had lost my life that night I would have gone to hell, but at this point I had no idea how I could possibly turn back to Jesus. I felt that I was too far gone. I knew the Bible and I knew that I had chosen to deny Him. I know now, of course, the truth is that no matter how far I try and run from the Father, He is always pursuing me. All it takes is for me to stop running and turn around - He is right there waiting with open arms.

BIRTH OF OUR FIRST CHILD

On the 18th of January 1992, we were excited to welcome our first baby into the world. Despite the fact that I had continued to use drugs and smoke throughout the entire pregnancy, our baby boy Joshua was born absolutely perfect - a testimony in itself of the miraculous power of God and His grace and mercy over us.

Once Josh was born, I again started thinking about the sort of life we were going to bring this child up in. Even though I was still hurt and angry at God and at those who were supposed to represent Him, I definitely didn't want my children to grow up living the way I was living now.

MOVING FROM ORANGE

April 1992.

When Joshua was just a couple of months old, he ended up very sick in hospital and we were told he had asthma. Even though I wasn't walking with the Lord at the time, I refused to accept the doctor's diagnosis. I told Mum, who prayed for him, and we decided to leave Orange and move to the Central Coast to be in a warmer climate. We didn't get any of the asthma medication that was suggested (puffers, etc.) and Josh has never had any more symptoms of asthma. Again, our Father in Heaven showed His faithfulness.

We moved to Newcastle in April 1992, where we lived for a few months before moving to the Central Coast. It didn't take long to get to know all the local drug dealers and didn't slow us down at all in our destructive lifestyle. In fact, it got worse.

CROP

If you have ever been addicted to drugs, you would know that you can never get enough. Although Lee was working full time (being paid cash in hand), we were both receiving government payments and we were involved in whatever it took to keep the supply coming in. We would often get lists from our suppliers of items they wanted, and we would get them for them by whatever means possible. We were also always borrowing money from our families and friends. There was never enough money, never enough drugs; it was just one vicious cycle, a merry-go-round, that we could not get off.

We found out that one of the dealers we knew had a crop growing nearby and we decided it would be easy enough to rip off. My father, who had never touched drugs in his life, heard what we were planning and said he would help (I thought that meant he would wait in the car, but he was little more involved than that!).

Although it is not a memory we are proud of, I will never forget standing by the road near the back of our station wagon with the boot open, watching my dad come running out of the bush with Lee carrying huge marijuana plants over their shoulders. Still a memory that makes me laugh today!

Obviously, Dad, having no idea and no real understanding of just how heavily addicted we were, thought he was helping (maybe saving money himself because of us "borrowing" all the time). When my mum saw them, she thought they were lovely looking plants!

BIRTH OF OUR SECOND CHILD

Thirteen months after our first child was born, on the 13th of February 1993, we welcomed our second child - a gorgeous baby girl, Amy. Again, I had continued to smoke and do drugs throughout the pregnancy, but again God had protected her little life. Lee and I were only twenty-six and twenty-one years old respectively, with two small children, living a life of drug addiction and involved in everything that lifestyle offers. It was starting to take its toll. We were constantly fighting with each other, and our children were growing up in an environment they didn't deserve. Our habits took centre stage and came first - before rent, bills, even food, and when we could not get our supplies, it'd be World War 3 in the house!

3

DIVINE INTERVENTION

M arch 1993.
An experience we will never forget also took place in the Blue Mountains of New South Wales. We were still living on the Central Coast and were travelling home after picking up a very large (and heavy) pump for a drilling rig, which was in the boot of our car - an old Holden Kingswood.

My dad was also travelling back at the same time, driving an M5 BMW. As we were driving through the winding roads in the mountains, Lee, who was racing my father, moved into the overtaking lane to go around Dad. As we were passing, the pump in the boot shifted and the back end of our car slid out so far that we were going sideways into two lanes of oncoming traffic. It seemed like slow motion; we had our two babies in the back and could do nothing to stop the inevitable accident.

Then, in an instant, it felt like the car was picked up and turned back around the right way. Put firmly back into our lane, we drove on, wondering what had just happened!

Divine intervention, divine protection, once again.

APPOINTMENT WITH GOD

April 1993.

Just one week after this miraculous incident in the mountains, we had an appointment with God.

We were totally dependent on drugs to get us through our daily lives, involved in crime, constantly arguing, with physical violence quite common. We had pretty much reached rock bottom. This was our life and it sucked.

Leaving the Social Security (now called Centrelink) building one morning after trying unsuccessfully to get an advance payment, we were on our way to the local dealer's place to get more drugs on credit. We had no fuel in the car and ran out of petrol on the way, right on the corner of the street where Phil and Julie Oldfield (now pastors of C3 Church in Tuggerah), lived. At the time they weren't pastors, but they were sold out for Jesus and the love of the Father flowed from their lives in a way that was tangibly felt.

I had known the Oldfields as a young teenager, and knew they were Christians. I reluctantly jumped out of the car and headed to their house with the express purpose of borrowing $10 for fuel to get us on our way to the dealer's house.

Remembering my previous experience of asking a Christian for $10, I was not very hopeful and not at all prepared for what would take place on this day.

When I knocked on the door Julie answered and was quite surprised to see me standing there. I immediately blurted out, "Hi! Long time-no-see. I've just ran out of fuel on the corner and was wondering if I could just borrow $10 to put fuel in the car?" Her response was, very gently, "Sure, if you tell me what happened to your eye." (At the time I had a black eye from a fight with Lee the night before).

I don't think it was what she said, or how she said it, it was more what I felt coming from her - no criticism, just concern. No judgement, just unconditional love. It was the presence of Jesus that I hadn't felt for so long. I burst into tears as she pulled me into her arms and just held me. Phil walked up the street to our car to chat with Lee and invited him to come down to the house.

That day changed our lives. Phil and Julie put aside whatever plans they had for the day and sat sharing the Gospel with us, praying with us, laughing with us, and crying with us. That day I recommitted my life to Jesus and Lee gave his life to Christ. We spent the whole day at their house. I have no idea what date it was, but I do remember we stayed for dinner and Julie made rice pudding for dessert! Demons were cast out of us, and freedom came as Phil and Julie poured everything into us they could, from the overflow of the Holy Spirit in their lives.

We were both totally delivered and set free from drug addiction that day and the change was immediate! We both physically felt the tangible presence of God so strongly; it was an undeniable encounter that changed our lives forever.

*Note: Thirty years after this, on Good Friday 2023, we were back on the Central Coast in C3 Tuggerah, the church Ps Phil and Julie pioneered. There we had the opportunity to tell their congregation the story and honour them both publicly. We are forever grateful for this beautiful couple and their family, for the way they represent the King, for the sacrifices they have made, for their passion for the lost and for their commitment to building the Kingdom of God. We honour you both and thank you for your continuous 'YES' to King Jesus!

SOLID FOUNDATION

May 1993.

Straight after our decision to follow Christ, our lives changed dramatically. From doing everything wrong, to being convicted, and wanting to do everything right! The car that we were driving was actually unregistered and Lee had lost his license a few months previously, so straight away the conviction of the Holy Spirit was at work, challenging us to do what was right. Now that our beliefs were based on scriptural truths, we had to apply these truths to our lives. It was no longer okay to drive an unregistered car or drive without a license. It was no longer okay to swear, it was no longer okay to steal, it was no longer okay to lie.

As we listened to the voice of the Lord and allowed Him to lead us, guide us and to discipline us, we found that we no longer wanted to do what was wrong, because we wanted to please Him. Just like our own children want to please us, we wanted to please our Heavenly Father.

Lee remembers how he would go to do the wrong thing and the Lord would gently speak to him saying, *"Don't do that son..."*

I was just so overwhelmed that the Lord still loved me. Despite the fact that I had turned my back on Him and walked away, His arms were open and ready to take me back in an instant.

As I mentioned in the previous chapter, we were totally delivered from drug addiction and had no desire to touch them again, but having lived in such a lifestyle for so long we needed to learn how to live out a normal Christian life. Our spirits were born again, but our flesh and our will and emotions still had a journey to go on. Our souls needed to be converted.

Phil and Julie had called a beautiful couple, Terry and Sue Moore, who were home group leaders in a local church at the time. The very next day after giving our lives to Jesus, Terry and Sue came to our house to help us set a foundation for the journey we had just begun. This amazing couple walked with us very closely for the next six months; for the first six weeks they came to our house every single evening to disciple us. They spent hours praying with us and for us, spending time in the Bible and teaching us, helping us and encouraging us. We are so grateful for their sacrifice, their love and faithfulness. They showed such commitment, which was so necessary to set a solid foundation for this incredible journey with God.

*Note: In late 2022, we also had the opportunity to catch up with Terry and Sue after nearly thirty years! It was so wonderful to thank them again after so long. They had no idea just how much they had helped us all those years ago. They simply loved God and loved people. They simply knew just how essential discipleship is for new believers.

Being discipled by Terry and Sue taught me some brilliant truths about foundations.

A solid foundation is the most important part of any building. Jesus shares the parable in the Gospels about the wise and foolish builder, *""Therefore whoever hears these sayings of Mine, and does them, I will liken him to a wise man who built his house on the rock: and the rain descended, the floods came, and the winds blew and beat on that house; and it did not fall, for it was founded on the rock. But everyone who hears these sayings of Mine, and does not do them, will be like a foolish man who built his house on the sand: and the rain descended, the floods came, and the winds blew and beat on that house; and it fell. And great was its fall."* (Matthew 7:24-27 NKJV)

When building a house (or any structure), the most important part is the foundation; the foundation is what holds the building up. The strength and stability of the house or structure lies in the foundation. It really doesn't matter what colour you paint the walls, if the foundation isn't right, the house will fall, especially when storms come.

I love this as a metaphor for our lives. Without a solid foundation in our Christian walk, we will easily be swayed. When temptations come, when trials come, when people let us down, when the enemy whispers lies in our ear, if our foundations aren't solid, we will fall. Knowing the truth of the God's Word and laying that as a foundation will impact every area of our lives.

Sometimes cracks appear in buildings after a time due to different circumstances like weather events and shifting ground. When this happens, we are often tempted to just fix the crack on the surface, but if we really want to make sure the structure is right, we should investigate the source of the problem. This could mean digging down, sometimes messing up the exterior a little before getting to the problem, making the adjustments, and then putting it back together again.

The same principles apply to our lives. If cracks start to appear, like for e.g., if sin starts to manifest in our lives. Or if our reactions or thoughts aren't right, if we are becoming offended or hard hearted, don't be afraid to mess up the exterior (take off the masks), honestly and openly re-examine and make the adjustments to the foundations that need to be made. Otherwise, we are fooling ourselves, we aren't living in the truth of the Word, and we aren't living in the victory and freedom that Christ paid for. We aren't living the life we were created for.

I have learnt that there are no shortcuts; we must take the time to build the foundation - read the Word and apply it to our life. Trust in the Lord and the promises of His Word. Grow in faith, hunger and thirst for righteousness. I know for sure that developing my prayer life - spending time in prayer and communion with God, building that intimate relationship with Him and learning to hear His voice, has been an essential part of building a strong foundation in my life.

The Bible says in John, *"My sheep know My voice...the voice of another they will not follow"*. A relationship with the Lord is the same as a relationship with others - the more time we spend with Him, the better we will know Him and the closer we will become. The more we discipline ourselves, abiding in Him and in His Word, worshipping and praying (which isn't just talking to Him but listening as well), the easier it will be to hear and know His voice.

We all need to build our own relationship with God, getting to know Him intimately. You can't spend time in the Word, in prayer, in the secret place without being changed by the power of His Spirit. Others can help guide, teach and direct us but they can't impart that relationship they have with the King. That's something that can only be cultivated by spending time with Him alone.

GETTING MARRIED

December 18, 1993.

A few months into our new journey with God, as He started to show us areas that needed to be changed or adjusted, we had a deep conviction to put things right in our living situation, which meant getting married! We had already lived together for over six years, had two gorgeous children, and planned to spend the rest of our lives together. So, on December 18, 1993, we were married in Redcliffe, Queensland, where we had recently moved.

ON FIRE

In Luke 7:47 it mentions that those who have been forgiven much, love much! Having had such a radical encounter with God and being instantly delivered and set free from addictions that had previously controlled our lives - we loved much! We were so excited and passionate to let everyone know about the One who had forgiven us!

We often tell the story of how Lee was banned from our children's day-care. From very early on in his walk with the Lord, Lee would hear God's voice not only speaking encouragement (and correction) to him, but also speaking to him about others (words of knowledge). One day, Lee was dropping our two small children off at day-care when he received a word of knowledge for one of the ladies working there. He gave her the word very passionately. It happened to be about her being a witch and that she needed to get out of the demonic situation she was in and come to Jesus. He spent about 10-15 minutes with her, she broke down crying and was visibly shaken by what God had revealed. Being young in the Lord, Lee wasn't really sure what to do next, so he said a quick prayer for her and left.

About an hour later I got a call from the day-care saying that Lee wasn't allowed back there. The word he had given was correct and they were freaking out! I went looking for him to deliver the message and found him at the Social Security building, (now called Centrelink), preaching to people outside!

Lee always says that no one told him he had to preach the Gospel and evangelise. No one sat him down and said, "now that you're saved, you will need to get other people saved!" It just came naturally.

When you are in love with someone, you can't help but talk about them. You are overflowing with love. I realise that this is a pretty bold statement to make, but I would question that someone has actually met Jesus and encountered Him, (actually experienced His forgiveness, His grace and mercy and His overwhelming love) if they never want to tell anybody about Him.

I like the example of a newly dating couple. When you are newly in love, everyone around you knows about it. You constantly want to be with each other and if you're apart, you are always talking about each other. That is first love. It's what the Bible talks about. When we are first saved, we are so in love with Jesus, so thankful that He saved us, so grateful that we are forgiven. We want to spend all our time in His presence, reading His Word, talking with Him, worshiping Him. Naturally the overflow of this time with Him would affect those around us because we would want them to experience Him also.

BABY NUMBER THREE

Three years into our walk with the Lord, we found ourselves expecting our third child. This was the first pregnancy that I did sober – no drugs, no alcohol, and our precious boy Jesse was born on October 8th, 1996, after just a 30-minute labour!

How different it now was to bring a baby into the world, a world where he would be raised to know and love God, instead of the destructive life we had lived before.

CHURCH LIFE

As we grew in our Christian walk, we also started serving in our local church wherever we were located.

We started by helping in the children's ministry when our children were young, and by the time they were in primary school, we were the children's ministry leaders in our local church. We had a church bus that went around picking children up from all around the local area to bring them to church (even though their parents didn't attend, they gave us permission to pick them up), and every few months we'd get the kids involved in putting on a special outreach and invite their parents too!

As our children got older, we grew with them and became youth group leaders. We also regularly held mid-week meetings in our home, were involved in different outreaches, and become event coordinators in the church.

Church attendance for our family isn't just about a box to tick on Sunday mornings. Church is family, it is doing life together with fellow believers, it is being trained and equipped, it is about serving and being planted – being part of a community so that we can flourish and grow. Just like we were before we were saved – we didn't just put our toes in. If we were in, we were ALL IN!

The same applied though once we started out in business.

BUSINESS VENTURES

2000.

At the beginning of our journey with the Lord, we began to learn about biblical principles which we started to put into practice, one of which was tithing.

Tithing is the one thing in the Bible that God says to test Him on. In Malachi it says, *"Bring all the tithes into the storehouse so there will be enough food in my Temple. If you do,"* says the Lord of Heaven's Armies, *"I will open the windows of heaven for you. I will pour out a blessing so great you won't have enough room to take it in! Try it! Put me to the test! Your crops will be abundant, for I will guard them from insects and disease. Your grapes will not fall from the vine before they are ripe,"* says the Lord of Heaven's Armies. *"Then all nations will call you blessed, for your land will be such a delight,"* says the Lord of Heaven's Armies."* (Malachi 3:10-12 NLT)

We started to give from the little we had and were amazed as the blessing of God started to pour out over us. The more we grew in this area, the more God showed His faithfulness. We have so many testimonies (some included in this book), of God's provision and blessing that is evident in our lives.

By the year 2000, we were able to purchase our first home, (which we renovated and sold just a few years later for more than double the price we bought it for).

In 2001 we were given the opportunity to purchase a small

amusement company, which we did in partnership with my dad. Over the next seven years we grew to be one of the biggest and best amusement companies on the Central Coast. We had, however, been working a lot on weekends and our attendance at church was really suffering. But when we did get there, we made sure we gave generously. We had also, by then, built a beautiful house on acreage on the Central Coast.

In 2007 we had the opportunity to purchase a drilling rig and decided to sell the amusement company to start a drilling company.

This decision took us on a journey that completely changed the course of our lives. The business went so well that we were soon earning more money than we'd ever made before. With just a quick prayer, but not much thought of what God wanted, we moved from New South Wales to Queensland to expand the business.

We know that *"all things work together for good for those who love God, to those who are the called according to His purpose."* We did love God, (although our first love fire was fading quickly), and we did know we were called for His purposes. We just hadn't figured out what those purposes were yet!

LUKEWARM

The drilling company became extremely successful. We had so much work we couldn't keep up. Lee often had to work away from home, but we were making so much money that the kids and I would often jump on a plane and join him wherever he happened to be in the country. Very similar to what my mother did with us when I was growing up.

Our church attendance had already started to decline when we were running the previous business, and our passion for the lost was becoming non-existent. Lee went from telling everyone he met about Jesus, to not wanting to even share that he was a Christian with clients, for fear of losing contracts.

When we did get to church though, we would continue to be generous with our finances thinking that this was enough, knowing deep down however, that it wasn't. We had become so lukewarm - we were so apathetic and complacent in our Christian walk. Our first love fire was barely even kindling, and the passion and heart for the lost was nearly non-existent.

> *Lukewarm Christian, you are one of the devils most power-ful weapons against the Gospel. When people look at you and the life you live and realise that your life is no different than theirs, they become convinced they don't need Jesus.*
> Daniel Kolenda

We are definitely not called to be lukewarm. Revelation 3:15-16 says, *"I know your works, that you are neither cold nor hot. I could wish you were cold or hot. So then, because you are lukewarm, and neither cold nor hot, I will vomit you out of My mouth."* Then in verse 19 it says, *"As many as I love, I rebuke and chasten. Therefore, be zealous and repent."*

I have often heard people who have been saved for several years and have "matured", saying things like "you just need to calm down", or "you're only new, the excitement will wear off". But we aren't meant to "calm down", the excitement isn't supposed to "wear off". We are meant to be ON FIRE!!

Burning Ones for the King of Kings!

I want to always keep that first love passion for our King Jesus and for those who are lost. It is not enough that I just go to church and at the same time live a distracted, unfocused and unintentional life, a life not fully lived for Him.

We were still attending church, still tithing, we even held regular connect group meetings in our home, but we were so distracted by the things of the world. Instead, our gaze, our attention should have been on Heaven, on Jesus.

The business had taken first place in our lives and everything else revolved around it. We were making enough money to do whatever we wanted, go wherever we wanted, buy whatever we wanted, and indeed, we were doing just that. There's nothing wrong with being in business, nothing wrong with being successful and making plenty of money, especially if that's what God has called you to do. But when that becomes number one, when it takes the place in your life where God should be, it can become as dangerous as the way we were living before we were saved.

As I write this and remember those days, I am reminded of the story in the Bible about a rich young ruler (Matthew 19:16-26). He asked Jesus what he must do to be saved. Jesus replied by reminding him of the Ten Commandments, to which the young ruler replied, *'I have kept all these since I was a boy'*. Jesus then told him to sell all he had and give the money to the poor, then come and follow Him. The rich young ruler's response was to walk away, saddened because he had so much, but wasn't willing to do as Jesus had asked. He wasn't willing to surrender everything, to put God first; he wasn't willing to leave all he had to follow Christ.

Jesus called his disciples the same way, *"And Jesus, walking by the Sea of Galilee, saw two brothers, Simon called Peter, and Andrew his brother, casting a net into the sea; for they were fishermen. Then He said to them, "Follow Me, and I will make you fishers of men." They immediately left their nets and followed Him. Going on from there, He saw two other brothers, James the son of Zebedee, and John his brother, in the boat with Zebedee their father, mending their nets. He called them, and immediately they left the boat and their father, and followed Him."* (Matthew 4:18-22)

How different their response was – they immediately left everything to follow Jesus.

At that time of our lives, we had definitely become like the rich young ruler. Our business had become number one.

Me-9 months

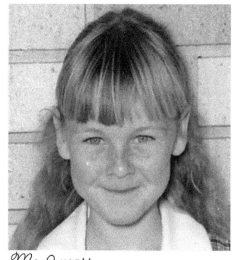

Me-9 years

Mum & I

Dad, my older sister Marie & I

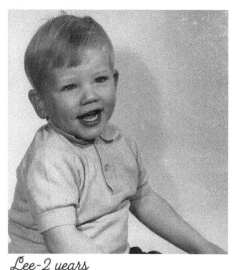

Lee-2 years

Lee-10 years

Lee 24 years, Me 19 years

Our firstborn, Joshua

Our Wedding

My Parents-Peter & Ann

Lee's Parents-Graham & Lois

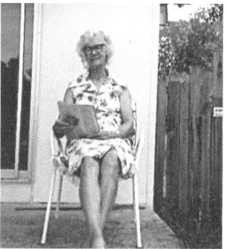

Nan Mary

Me-17 years, Lee 22 years

Lee & I-early days with Lee's family

4

DEATH INTERRUPTS

DAD

May 28, 2010.

The year 2010 started out great. In April we had a big family holiday in Coffs Harbour with our children, my parents, and my sister and brother-in-law, who were expecting their first baby.

Just one month after that, on the 28th of May, we received a phone call from my mum saying that my dad had just been killed in a truck accident on the other side of the country. I felt like my world had suddenly fallen apart. I was absolutely devastated. Dad was my mate. We spoke nearly every day about everything and anything!

Dad was also in the drilling business at the time and was in Perth, Western Australia, for work. The evening before he died, he had called my mother to let her know they had just secured a massive contract with Rio Tinto. He had worked hard all his life to provide for his family and was brilliant at what he did. He had established multiple businesses from the ground up and he could design and build anything he put his mind to. Dad was so excited about the contract. This was what he had worked for. They would be set for life, millionaires in fact! The next morning, he was dead.

On the night I received the call that my dad had died, for the first time in 17 years all I wanted was drugs. I just wanted to wipe myself out and pretend this wasn't even happening. I had every intention of doing just that, but God protected me. When I am weak, He is strong. His grace is sufficient. I literally felt His presence carry me through the next six months.

I had to take care of all Dad's business affairs, making sure Mum was looked after. This meant being away from the family for quite a few months, running Dad's business for a short time, then collecting trucks, rigs and equipment from all over the country and finally selling the assets and closing down his business.

I never really had time to grieve, but every day I felt a physical ache in my heart. When those you love leave this earth, eternity becomes so much more real to you, as does the choice we all have to make of where we will spend eternity – heaven or hell. Eternally with God, or eternally separated from Him.

We all know that the one certainty, the one thing we will all have to face, the one reality of life, is death. We are not promised tomorrow. We cannot ever guarantee another day. But I love that only God knows the number of our days. *"Your eyes have seen my unformed substance; And in Your book were all written the days that were appointed for me, when as yet there was not one of them [even taking shape]."* (Psalms 139:16 AMP)

At the time of Dad's death, we had just started running a connect group in our home and we were studying the book "Live before You Die" by Daniel Kolenda. How much more did this mean to me now. The certainty of death was all the more real to me (unless the Lord returns for us first), but was I actually living?! I might be going through the motions - eat, work, sleep, repeat, but was I really living?

The Bible says that Jesus came to bring life and life more abundantly. God has a plan for every single one of us. All our days are written in His book. Am I living out what He has written? It's completely up to me. I can choose to follow His plan or run my own race.

CRAIG

January 2011.

In 2011 things were becoming the new normal (life without Dad). We were still running our own business, which was busier than ever, although my heart really wasn't in it. Our family was different, but the world doesn't just stop.

Our eldest son was now working for us full time. We were in the middle of planning for our daughter's wedding, which was just a few weeks away. Then, on January 24th, 2011, Lee and I were woken with the news that one of Lee's brothers had died of a heart attack during the night.

All the heartache came flooding back, all the grief of losing someone so close, the absolute devastation for the family that were left without a dad and husband, a son and a brother, an uncle and a dearly loved friend.

We were really starting to question what we should be doing. We had never gone back to finish the "Live Before You Die" book, but it was certainly in our minds. We could make all the money in the world, but were we living the life that God had purposed for us?

DANIEL

March 26, 2011.

Just one month after we had buried Lee's brother, before we could catch our breath, we got a phone call from a very close friend, saying that our best mate Daniel had just been shot and killed in a tattoo parlour in Sydney.

We had known Daniel and his family for years and he was more like a brother than a friend. We had shared houses; our kids grew up together and we had worked together in our business. Although we had spent our drug days together, we had also had the privilege of leading Daniel to the Lord a couple of years after we were saved.

Again, we were devastated. We had spoken to him just a few weeks before, when he had called to send his love for the loss of Lee's brother.

We are also very close to Daniel's sisters and his mum. They asked Lee if he would speak at the funeral, which he agreed to do. By this stage we had had enough - the truth of eternity was burning in our hearts. The reality that we all have to choose where we will spend eternity. The fact that we could make all the money in the world, but it couldn't buy our salvation (or that of our friends and family). The fire was starting to rekindle, and Lee decided that he would share the Gospel at the funeral.

The funeral was attended by quite a number of bikies from a well-known outlaw motorcycle club and the President of the club planned to speak as well. Lee got up first and shared a simple Gospel message. He explained how Daniel had given his life to Christ and we believed that he was now in Glory with his Saviour Jesus! The President was the next one to speak, but was visibly in shock by what Lee had shared. He stood up and said, "I was going to say a whole heap of stuff, but I guess the main thing is that Daniel is now with God." He then went and sat down.

After the funeral we had the opportunity to share the gospel and pray with quite a few of the gang members. While we may never see the fruit, we know without a shadow of doubt that many seeds were sown that day.

I am reminded of the verse that says, *"I assure you and most solemnly say to you, unless a grain of wheat falls into the earth and dies, it remains alone [just one grain, never more]. But if it dies, it produces much grain and yields a harvest."* (John 12:24 AMP)

We are so grateful that we had the chance to sow those seeds, and while we mourn the loss of a precious friend, we pray that his death and the deaths of my father and Lee's brother yield a mighty harvest for the Kingdom.

Last family holiday with Dad

My Dad

Lee's brother Craig

Lee & Craig

Lee & I with Daniel & his family

Daniel Vella

5

LET'S BUY A TENT!

A pril 2011.
Midway through 2011 I felt like I was living on the edge, constantly waiting for the next phone call, the next bad thing to happen. Business continued as usual and we were making quite a lot of money, but our focus had definitely shifted. We were so much more aware of the frailty of life, of how quickly it can all be over, and the reality of where people would spend eternity.

We were remembering how passionate we had been when we first gave our lives to the Lord, and we realised just how lukewarm we had become. But the fire was starting to burn again.

One Sunday morning our pastor, Mike Warman, preached about following our God-given dreams and pursuing the calling on our lives. He called me out for prayer at the end of the service and spoke prophetically over me. The only things I remember him saying were that there are no more 'dark scary monsters' around the next corner (which is exactly what I was dreading), and to stop looking back but to look forward and focus on where God was leading us.

I had such an incredible encounter with God, and I cried A LOT (for the first time since my dad had died).

When we got home that day, I sat in my office in front of the computer and googled "one-thousand-man tent for sale". Don't ask me what made me do that, but it was obviously God, because we had never even thought about buying a tent.

Right at the very top of the results page of the Google search was *"For sale - The Tent of Promise".*

I remembered the prophetic words that were given to me when I was young, and I knew this was what we were meant to do.

I walked into the lounge room where Lee was and said, "I think we should buy a big tent and travel around Australia preaching the Gospel." Lee replied, "You are crazy!" He thought I had lost my mind after all the trauma of the last twelve months!

I persisted; once the idea was in my head, I knew it was from God. I took a girlfriend with me to meet with the owners of the tent, Barry and Sandra Cunnington, told them that I wanted to buy it and said that I'd be back once the Lord had spoken to Lee. A few weeks later, Lee agreed to meet with Barry and Sandra. It was at that meeting that Barry let us know there were other people wanting to buy the tent, but he felt the Lord wanted us to have it. He told Lee to pray about it and let him know what we decide.

We prayed. We had others pray. We prayed some more and felt the Lord really wanted us to have it. Just to be certain, we put some conditions in place on the sale and asked the Lord that if it really was His will, the current owners would agree to every condition.

One of the conditions was the price, and another was that we would take the tent straight away and pay it off over a period of time. All our money was tied up in the business and we had no way of accessing it to buy a big Gospel tent. We knew there were other people wanting to buy the tent who had the finances ready to go. Nevertheless, we put our conditions to the owners and waited. They had already been in prayer with their team and knew it was God's plan. Within the week they had agreed, and the tent was ours!

Along with the tent, we purchased a huge truck, a small bus, a caravan and an enclosed storage trailer, which we later turned into a food van.

INTRODUCTION TO TENT MINISTRY

August 2011.

Once we had the tent in our possession, we wasted no time planning outreaches to reach the lost! Despite never having actually preached and having had no training to do this whatsoever, we knew this was what God wanted us to do. Not the kind of people to start with something small, we jumped right in and organised a 12-week tour to start off, going to six different cities. We invited some friends over from the United Sates, who also brought an awesome team to travel with us. We put our eldest son in charge of our business, which had months of already contracted work ahead. We thought this would be an awesome financial support for the ministry. The convoy set off with Lee driving the huge Mack truck, a coaster bus with the team from the USA, my car towing our caravan with myself, our youngest son and my mother, and our heavily pregnant daughter and grandson in their car.

Two hours into the trip, the Mack truck in which we had just installed a brand-new motor, started having trouble. Lee already started having doubts, until he heard God speak to him and say, *"if it was for the business, you would get the truck there."* So, he did. He made some adjustments, he persevered, he prayed and by late that evening we all arrived safely in Orange, a few weeks before the first crusade was to start. It was the middle of winter and was freezing cold and snowing!! (We clearly hadn't thought too much about tent meetings and the weather in Orange!). Our daughter's husband joined us after a week and our new granddaughter was born in Orange just before the outreach started.

Because it was so cold, we ordered some gas jet heaters to be sent up from Sydney to warm the tent and one of the local pastors offered to pay for the first week's gas. The very first night of the outreach the tent was packed. It was snowing outside but the heaters made it warm enough in the tent to wear a t-shirt! After the first week however, we found out that it cost $1500 to keep the tent warm, and we had to pay the bill the following week!

The second week of the crusade, our brand-new granddaughter got whooping cough, which is very dangerous for a brand-new baby, so she ended up in ICU in hospital and was very sick. We wanted to go and support them, as our daughter and her husband had travelled back to Brisbane by this time. But they insisted that we stay in Orange and continue with the outreach. So, we prayed.

Just as we were nearing the end of the second week, Lee went to pick up my mum so that she could attend the evening meeting and found her lying half paralysed on her bed. She had an excruciating headache and Lee picked her up, carried her to the car, and was about to rush her to the hospital when she said, "Get me to the tent!"

He quickly drove her to the tent and carried her inside where we all gathered round and prayed for her, before calling for an ambulance. She spent the night in hospital, was told she had a brain bleed (stroke), but was nevertheless discharged the following day after what can only be described as a miraculous recovery!

During that second week of meetings, we also received a call from our son with some bad news. The major contracts we had lined up to bring in income while we travelled had all been cancelled! This was something that had never happened before. We had no other source of income!

We were still in the first city of a six-city tour. People were getting saved, people were being healed, people were encountering God and being set free, but we were beginning to question God. Our assumption was that because we were now working for Him, everything should be amazing. But while He was moving powerfully in the meetings, we seemed to be getting attacked from all directions.

It was time to learn and grow!

OUR SWORD FOR THE BATTLE

When you enter a boxing ring, you should expect your opponent to fight back. The thing we need to remember as sons and daughters of King Jesus, is that we are not the ones who enter the ring! Jesus has already defeated the enemy. He has already won the fight. The enemy is not at all happy because we don't fight FOR victory, we fight FROM victory! Jesus has already won the war; we just need to trust Him and walk in that victory.

Paul describes this amazing victory that Jesus has won for us in Romans 8:31-39:

"What then shall we say to these things? If God is for us, who can be against us?

He who did not spare His own Son, but delivered Him up for us all, how shall He not with Him also freely give us all things?

Who shall bring a charge against God's elect? It is God who justifies.

Who is he who condemns? It is Christ who died, and furthermore is also risen, who is even at the right hand of God, who also makes intercession for us.

Who shall separate us from the love of Christ? Shall tribulation, or distress, or persecution, or famine, or nakedness, or peril, or sword? As it is written: "For Your sake we are killed all day long; We are accounted as sheep for the slaughter." Yet in all these things we are more than conquerors through Him who loved us.

For I am persuaded that neither death nor life, nor angels nor principalities nor powers, nor things present nor things to come, nor height nor depth, nor any other created thing, shall be able to separate us from the love of God which is in Christ Jesus our Lord."

What an incredible passage of scripture!

We will absolutely come up against the enemy. We are in a battle, but precious Jesus, our Saviour, has already conquered the enemy and is now interceding for us. The Word promises that NOTHING can separate us from His love and that we are MORE than conquerors through HIM! We can stand on this truth, confident and without fear, no matter what happens!

Another important thing the team and Lee and I had to constantly remember was that our battle is not against human beings or things we can see, but against elements of the unseen world. Ephesians 6:12-18 reminds us that the fight is not against flesh and blood but against principalities and powers of the unseen realm. It speaks of the full armour of God. In verse 10 it says to *"be strong in the Lord and the power of His might"*. This is the key to understanding the armour of God - all the pieces belong to Him and come from Him. All these gifts God gives us are us for our defence. All are designed to help us stand against the enemy.

Belt of Truth – this is the very first piece of the armour to put on. The Bible says that Jesus is the Way, the Truth and the Life (John 14:6). He alone is the Truth. Without Him the rest of the armour would be useless.

The belt of a Roman soldier was a thick heavy leather strap that held the soldier's sword. The belt of truth in the armour of God holds the Sword of the Spirit, linking truth and the Word of God!

Breastplate of Righteousness - 2 Corinthians 5:21 says, *"For He made Him who knew no sin to be sin for us, that we might become the righteousness of God in Him."*

The breastplate of the Roman soldier was made of bronze or chain, it protected the heart and other vital organs, and it was attached to the belt. We have been made righteous only through Christ. To put on the breastplate of righteousness we must first have on the belt of truth. Without it, we will be relying on our own attempt at righteousness, which is described as *'filthy rags'* in Isaiah 64:6.

Shoes of the Gospel of Peace - having our feet firmly planted so that we can stand strong, holding our ground remembering that our position in Christ is not based on our own abilities or worthiness, but on the truth of God's word and what Jesus Christ has won for us through His birth, death and resurrection. As well as standing our ground, shoes are also for advancing. We are commissioned to *"Go into all the world and preach the gospel."* (Mark 16:15), the Bible says in Isaiah 52:7, *"How beautiful upon the mountains are the feet of him who brings* *good news, who proclaims peace, who brings glad tidings of good things, who proclaims salvation!"*

Shield of Faith -The Roman shield of the time was as large as a door and covered the warrior completely. It is vitally important and provides protection against the lies (fiery darts) of the enemy.

"Faith is the confidence of things hoped for and the evidence of things not seen ...it is impossible to please God without faith." (Hebrews 11:1 and 6)

Sometimes the attacks of the enemy cause us to doubt, but faith prompts us to believe.

Faith reminds us that although we may not see the victory, God is true to His word. Faith is the protective barrier between us and the attack of the enemy.

Helmet of Salvation - The assurance of our salvation is an impenetrable defence against anything the enemy tries to throw at us. Because of the power of the cross, the enemy no longer has any hold on us, and he knows that. The problem arises when we don't know that, when we allow the doubts, the lies, the confusion into our minds. And so, we must keep the helmet of salvation firmly tightened so that we can, *"cast down arguments and every high thing that exalts itself against the knowledge of God, bringing every thought into captivity to the obedience of Christ,"* (2 Corinthians 10:5).

We can do this by:

- renewing our minds,
- allowing the truth of God's word to be our focus,
- rejecting doubt and
- remembering that the victory has already been won.

Sword of the Spirit - this is the only piece of armour that is used on the offensive. The Word of God is the only weapon we need to attack the enemy. The Word of God in our mouths is just as powerful as the Word of God in His mouth because Christ lives in us!

The Word of God is the source:

- for our faith - *"So then faith comes by hearing, and hearing by the word of God."* Romans 10:17.
- of victory over sin - *"Your word I have hidden in my heart, that I might not sin against You."* Psalms 119:11.
- of healing - *"My child, pay attention to what I say. Listen carefully to my words. Don't lose sight of them. Let them penetrate deep into your heart, for they bring life to those who find them, and healing to their whole body."* Proverbs 4:20-22.
- of guidance - *"Your word is a lamp unto my feet and a light to my path."* Psalm 119:105
- of preparation and equipping - *"All Scripture is given by inspiration of God, and is profitable for doctrine, for re-proof, for correction, for instruction in righteousness, that the man of God may be complete, thoroughly equipped for every good work."* 2 Timothy 3:16-17.
- of purity and holiness - *"How can a young man stay pure? Only by living in the Word of God and walking in its truth."* Psalms 119:9 (TPT). It is how we examine ourselves - *"For the word of God is living and powerful, and sharper than any two-edged sword, piercing even to the division of soul and spirit, and of joints and marrow, and is a discerner of the thoughts and intents of the heart."* (Hebrews 4:12)

I cannot emphasise enough the importance of spending time in the Word of God. It is our manual for life. It is our daily bread!

In my early days of walking with the Lord, as a young teen, one habit I formed very quickly was reading the Word. I have mentioned in other parts of this book that my Bible from those years is barely held together and has notes written in everywhere, and verses highlighted!

When I came back to the Lord as a young mum, the ability to spend that same amount of time in the Word was challenging. Trying to juggle children, a household, later running businesses and even now, in full time minis-try, it can be challenging to make sure I am spending enough time in the Word. However, knowing that just as much as I need food for my body, I also need spiritual food, encourages me to prioritise a daily devotional time.

Reading whole books of the Bible, doing studies on different people, reading it from cover to cover or studying different subjects, are just some ways I have learnt over the years to study and read the Bible. The most important thing is that we make it a habit; start off with just a verse a day, then a small chapter, working your way towards an amount that works for you daily.

One book I read in Bible College that I found helpful was called, *Them, Us, and Me: How the Old Testament Speaks to People Today* by Jacqueline Grey. This book helped me understand how to read the word in the con-text of what it related to at the time it was written, what it means to us now and how I can apply it to my own life daily.

As a mum, reading and learning Bible stories with my children was (and still is) a regular practice.

THE THREE P'S

In our ministry and in our business Lee and I always needed to know three important things. 1. That God is our provision. 2. That God is our protection, and 3. Our true identity is found in Jesus Christ. These three things are essential if we are to live the life that God intended for us. Some examples of our Heavenly Father's provision and protection over our lives are included in this book, but there have been so many times, throughout our lives, when God has supplied our needs and protected us from harm. Some we probably don't even know about or even acknowledge that it was the Lord.

We have to know our true identity - that we are first and foremost sons and daughters of God, the King of the universe. When I walk out my journey knowing WHO I am and WHOSE I am, I walk in His favour and in victory. I am confident that no matter what I face each day, in every situation, I am a child of God.

After Jesus' baptism, He was led into the wilderness to be tempted.

We read in Matthew 4 that these are the same three things that the enemy used to challenged Jesus:

1. **Provision** (Matthew 4:2-4) - While our plan when stepping out into the ministry was to keep our business going to support us and cover expenses, God had other plans and we needed to quickly realise that we are not the true supplier of our needs - God is. How can we teach faith if we haven't lived it, how can we know that God is Jehovah Jireh (our Provider), if we aren't trusting Him for the provision we need? Philippians 4:19 says, *"My God shall supply all your needs according to His riches in glory in Christ Jesus."*
   One year, we sat down and added up all our income for the year, and all our expenses and found that the expenditures far outweighed the income. This was supernatural provision!

2. **Protection** (Matthew 4:5-7) - Even when the enemy is throwing everything he can at you, God has the last word. While all these things were being thrown at us from every direction at the start of our tent ministry, God's hand was always protecting us and our family. By the time we got to the second city of the tour, we had received news from our daughter that our granddaughter was out of hospital and out of danger.
   The word of God promises His protection. He is always faithful, *"But the Lord is faithful. He will establish and guard you against the evil one."* (Thessalonians 3:3.)

3. **Position** (Matthew 4:8-10) - In the same way the enemy came and said to Adam and Eve in the garden that if they ate of the fruit on a particular tree, they would become like God. The fact was, though, they were already like God; they were created in His image. Their enemy made them doubt and forget their true identity.

Before I knew my identity in Christ as a young teen, I would try to find love and acceptance in so many other ways. This led me to the destructive path that I journeyed on for many years, with relationships, drugs, alcohol, crime; whatever I could do to try and find out who I was and to be accepted by those I surrounded myself with.

Once I had reached the end of that journey and re-dedicated my life to Christ, in some ways the change was instant, but it was still a process to know exactly who I was IN HIM! To understand that I was forgiven and loved unconditionally, that I was now accepted for who I was (who He had made me to be), not for what I did, or didn't, do. It was a process to know that I have authority over the enemy and that I can walk in the victory that Jesus bought for me.

Even when I stepped into ministry, I realised along the way that even if I never preached another message or held another outreach, God would love me just the same. There is nothing I can do to make Him love me more and nothing I can do to make Him love me any less. I am His beloved.

Discovering my identity could only be accomplished by spending time with our Saviour and by meditating on the truths in His Word - that He created me and He knows me (Psalm 139), **that I am forgiven** (Ephesians 1:7), **I am loved** (Ephesians 2:4-5), **I am chosen, holy and blameless** (Ephesians 1:4), **I am more than a conqueror** (Romans 8:37), **I am victorious** (1 Corinthians 15:57), **I am complete in Him** (Colossians 2:10), **I am redeemed** (Ephesians 1:7), **I am justified** (Romans 5:1),so many more. The Bible is FULL of truths about our identity. If we meditate on these, if we confess them, if we believe them and allow them to shape us, we will walk confidently and secure in who we are as children of the King.

The enemy will always try to make you doubt the provision and protection of God and your position or your identity as a son or daughter of God. But *"Let us hold fast the confession of our faith without wavering, for He who promised is faithful."* (Hebrews 10:23)

YOU CAN'T GIVE WHAT YOU HAVEN'T GOT

After two weeks of tent meetings, we packed up in Orange and headed to our next city, Canberra! On arrival, we set up the tent again, ready for the next two weeks. But the very first evening we just felt flat. We had poured out so much of our heart and soul in Orange.

Every night we had prayed with people. Each day we would be doing evangelism training and ministering on the streets. So, on that very first night in Canberra, the whole team lay down on the altar, realising that we couldn't do this in our own strength. We needed to be filled and re-filled ourselves!

We learnt very quickly that we had to make sure we were spending that personal time with Jesus; time in worship, time in prayer, time reading the Bible and meditating on it. Even though we were in corporate meetings every night, if we weren't spending time ourselves in that secret place with Him, we would soon have nothing to give.

I have learnt that I can't rely on corporate worship, church services, revival meetings or large gatherings to sustain my relationship with the Lord. Many times, throughout the book of Acts, the disciples were again "filled" with the spirit (Acts 2:2-4, Acts 4:8, Acts 4:31, Acts 7:55, Acts 9:17, Acts 13:9)

Even Jesus withdrew to be alone and pray. If He needed that time alone with the Father in the secret place, how much more do we need time in that secret place with Him. (Luke 5:16, Matthew 14:13, Luke 6:12-13, Luke 22:39-44)

> *"The public touch has got to turn into a private kiss - or it will all fade away. The reason He gives you the public touch is to draw you to the private kiss."*
> Eric Gilmour

We all like the fire, the excitement, the revival, but sometimes God is in the gentle whisper. There is a Biblical account of how God is found speaking to Elijah in a still, small voice, *"Then He said, 'Go out, and stand on the mountain before the Lord.' And behold, the Lord passed by, and a great and strong wind tore into the mountains and broke the rocks in pieces before the Lord, but the Lord was not in the wind; and after the wind an earthquake, but the Lord was not in the earthquake; and after the earthquake a fire, but the Lord was not in the fire; and after the fire a still small voice. So it was, when Elijah heard it, that he wrapped his face in his mantle and went out and stood in the entrance of the cave. Suddenly a voice came to him, and said, 'What are you doing here, Elijah?'"* (1 Kings 19:11-13 NKJV).

When we're in revival (when God is pouring out His Spirit in a way that is beyond what we experience on a regular Sunday service, when we're seeing salvations and miracles breaking out beyond the four walls of the church building, when we're seeing the body of Christ working in unity to see their cities impacted by the Gospel), our attention must stay on Jesus, focusing on His Face, not His hand. Fixing our gaze on Him, not on the miracles or the manifestations, not on the anointing moving through you or others but on the One Who is the source of that anointing. I never take for granted the glory, the power, the beauty, but my highest calling is to seek Him!

And so, we had to learn to give from the overflow; *"out of our innermost being will flow rivers of living water"* (John 7:38). When we're ministering to others, which we should all be doing in some way or another if we know Jesus, we need to remain full ourselves and to give out of the overflow.

We always have to maintain that precious intimate relationship with our Saviour, keeping short accounts with Him and keeping the fire of our first love burning.

"Be enthusiastic to serve the Lord, keeping your passion toward him boiling hot! Radiate with the glow of the Holy Spirit and let him fill you with excitement as you serve him. Let this hope burst forth within you, releasing a continual joy. Don't give up in a time of trouble, but commune with God at all times." (Romans 12:11-12 TPT)

Also, let's make sure that we are living right in our character, our actions, our choices, *"work out your own salvation with fear and trembling"* (Philippians 2:12).

Whilst we are continually giving and ministering, it's important to make sure that we don't disqualify ourselves, that we live disciplined lives so that we can persevere and run the race to the end, always practicing what we preach.

"Do you not know that those who run in a race all run, but one receives the prize? Run in such a way that you may obtain it. And everyone who competes for the prize is temperate in all things. Now they do it to obtain a perishable crown, but we for an imperishable crown. Therefore, I run thus: not with uncertainty. Thus I fight: not as one who beats the air. But I discipline my body and bring it into subjection, lest, when I have preached to others, I myself should become disqualified." (1 Corinthians 9:24-27 NKJV)

ORPHAN OR SON

One of the most important revelations we need before we even venture into what we feel God calling us to, is that we know our identity in Him.

I mentioned previously that when Jesus was tested in the wilderness, there were three things that He was challenged on - provision, protection and position.

Position is all about our identity.

Ask yourself this question: Do I think and act like an orphan or like a son or daughter of God?

An orphan is someone who has no known mother or father. Do we know our Heavenly Father? Do we really know Him? Do we have a relationship with Him? Do we feel His passionate love for us? Do we hear His heartbeat, what He cares about?

Knowing our identity in Christ, who we are as a much-loved son or daughter of the King, is one of the most powerful weapons we have against the enemy. It is also the most secure place we can be.

When we know who we are in Christ and Whose we are, when we know the authority that we carry because we're a child of the Most High, when we know that our Father God is a good Father - we are protected, we are confident, we are shielded, we are guarded, we are stead-fast, we are sheltered, we are certain and we are immovable.

When we really understand our position in Christ, who we are IN HIM, it changes the way we think and live.

- **We become a new person**. *"This means that anyone who belongs to Christ has become a new person. The old life is gone; a new life has begun!"* (2 Corinthians 5:17)
- **We are loved unconditionally, forever.** As Jesus came out of the water when He was baptised, God the Father spoke aloud saying, *"This is My beloved Son, in whom I am well pleased!"* (Matthew 3:17). Before Jesus had preached, before He had healed the sick or raised the dead, before He had done anything, the Father was well pleased with Him.

  We don't need to earn Gods love, He loves us!! As a parent, my children don't need to do anything to deserve my love or to earn my love. There is nothing they can do that will make me love them any more (or any less). How much more does our Heavenly Father love us?

  "See how very much our Father loves us, for he calls us his children, and that is what we are..." (1 John 3:1 NLT)
- **We love because He loved us first.** An orphan will constantly be working or serving, trying to gain acceptance or approval, but a son or daughter will be serving out of love for the Father.

  An orphan will be insecure and jealous of his brothers or sisters, but a son or daughter will cheer others on, so that they too will walk in the fullness of all the Lord has for them.
- **We are humble and peaceful.** An orphan will strive, struggle and fight to achieve success...a son or daughter will remain in stead-fast peace that only comes from the place of abiding in Christ while walking where He leads.
- **We have a transformed mind**. In the story of the prodigal son, after he had squandered all the money and found himself at the very bottom (literally in the pigpen), the Bible says, *"When he finally came to his senses"* (Luke 15:17). The orphan mentality is often a mindset that needs to be broken. We need to take authority

over this mindset and come into agreement with the truth of the word of God that says, *"I will not leave you as orphans"* (John 14:18). We are sons and daughters of the King of kings, we are a royal priesthood, a holy nation, a people belonging to God. We are chosen, we are called, we are accepted, we are loved.

When we enter into what He has called us to from THIS place, we will be unstoppable. It won't matter if we have the approval or the affirmation of man, because everything we do is for an audience of One.

"But those who know their God will be strong and do great exploits." (Daniel 11:32)

God is raising up a people who will know Him intimately, who will be transformed into His image by beholding Him, and who will demonstrate mighty acts to manifest His power for the glory of His Name.

We cannot be serving the Lord to gain favour or out of obligation, or to try to make up for where we may have fallen short.

Serving Him should only come out of the place of intimacy and love, knowing our identity.

At the same time, we maintain our integrity - making sure we are keeping a check on ourselves, on our own hearts and our own thoughts; making sure our morals remain in place and we are not being tempted or falling into sin; making sure we are honest with ourselves and others. When we keep watch over these things, we will have the most influence and impact on those around us.

Intimacy, Identity, Integrity, Influence, Impact!

We cannot base our identity on our performance or service to the Lord or be serving Him to gain acceptance. We are already accepted, and our identity is based on the truth of who God says we are.

It is not in this order: 1.performance (serving), 2.identity, 3.acceptance.

It is in this order: 1.acceptance, 2.identity, 3.performance.

SURPRISE BABY!!

October 2013.

About eighteen months into our ministry journey, we got a wonderful surprise. At forty years of age, I found out I was expecting our fourth child, seventeen years after our third!

Once I'd gotten over the shock of it, I only prayed one thing - that if God wanted us to continue in ministry, this baby had better travel well! He certainly answered my prayers. On October 11th Kari Grace joined our family and two weeks later we were holding a tent crusade (our second time back in Orange) where she was dedicated in one of the meetings. She has travelled all over Australia, and even around the world with us since then, and loves it!

IMPALED

December 2014.

One memory we will never forget was from 2014. It was our last tent crusade for the year, just before Christmas. We were in beautiful Port Macquarie with the tent set up right next to the beach! We'd had an awesome week with salvations, healings, people delivered and set free, and even baptisms in the ocean. God had moved powerfully.

Lee and a couple of the guys on the team were packing up the tent. Lee went into the back of the truck with one of the three phase power boxes and climbed the ladder to hang it up on the hooks, but as he was trying to hang it, he lost his footing and fell off the ladder. On the way down he impaled his arm on the hook!

Lee suffered such a horrendous injury that he ended up spending a lot of time in and out of hospital over the next few weeks.

Nevertheless, Gods protection was still so evident. When the surgeons operated, they were amazed that the hook had missed every muscle, every nerve, and every artery in his arm by millimetres!

Throughout our lives we have seen and experienced so many testimonies of salvations, healings and miracles, but there are also many stories of tough times, stretching times, times when people have betrayed us or let us down, times when sickness and death have affected us or those we love, financial difficulties, hurt, loss and pain.

The Bible says, *"Many are the afflictions of the righteous, but the Lord delivers him out of them all."* (Psalms 34:19 NKJV)

Often, we are happy to serve God when things are going well, when there are no tests or trials, but when things come against us, when we are going through hard times (which we will), we grumble and complain, we cry out to God and ask "Why?".

The Word says to *"count it all joy"* (James 1:2 NKJV), when we go through these trials because it is then that we are faced with a choice - to allow ourselves to grow or to shrink back. The Passion Translation puts it this way, *"My fellow believers, when it seems as though you are facing nothing but difficulties, see it as an invaluable opportunity to experience the greatest joy that you can! For you know that when your faith is tested it stirs up in you the power of endurance. And then as your endurance grows even stronger, it will release perfection into every part of your being until there is nothing missing and nothing lacking."*

Sometimes the Lord is wanting to discipline us, to develop our character, to mature us, even to protect us, just as we would our own children as they are growing up. It may not be fun or enjoyable at the time, but it is so necessary for our growth!

"And you have forgotten the exhortation which speaks to you as to sons: 'My son, do not despise the chastening of the Lord, Nor be discouraged when you are rebuked by Him; For whom the Lord loves He chastens, And scourges every son whom He receives'. If you endure chastening, God deals with you as with sons; for what son is there whom a father does not chasten? But if you are without chastening, of which all have become partakers, then you are illegitimate and not sons. Furthermore, we have had human fathers who corrected us, and we paid them respect. Shall we not much more readily be in subjection to the Father of spirits and live? For they indeed for a few days chastened us as seemed best to them, but He for our profit, that we may be partakers of His holiness. Now no chastening seems to be joyful for the present, but painful;

nevertheless, afterward it yields the peaceable fruit of righteousness to those who have been trained by it." (Hebrews 12:5-11 NKJV).

We all enjoy the blessings and the goodness of God over our lives. We all want the anointing, the power, and the fire of the Holy Spirit, but are we willing to allow God to work in us? Are we willing to receive persecution? Are we willing to be obedient? Are we ALL IN or are we only in for the good times?

Philippians 3:10 says, *"that I may know Him and the power of His resurrection, and the fellowship of His sufferings, being conformed to His death,"*

If we want the fire, are we ready for the suffering?

"Yet if anyone suffers as a Christian, let him not be ashamed, but let him glorify God in this matter."

(I Peter 4:16)

"For I consider that the sufferings of this present time are not worthy to be compared with the glory which shall be revealed in us." (Romans 8:18)

Are we ready to be obedient to what He asks of us? Are we willing to be purified so that we can carry His anointing? We all have things in our lives we need to deal with along the way, lessons we need to learn.

FAITH ISN'T FAITH UNTIL IT'S TESTED!

Trusting God requires us to risk the life we have for the life He's promised. As I mentioned, when starting the tent ministry our plan was to keep our business to finance the ministry; Gods plan, however, was very different.

Hebrews 11:1 and 6 says, *"Now faith is the substance of things hoped for, the evidence of things not seen ... And without faith it is impossible to please God."*

Faith requires obedience, trust, sacrifice, action, patience, focus. Faith requires that you stand, regardless of your circumstances, regardless of the pressures of this world, regardless of the accusation of the enemy. Faith that isn't tested is weak and ineffective. We need to exercise our faith just like we would exercise our muscles to build them up.

Even though our circumstances may look different, the word of God is the final truth. By faith we have been saved, by faith we have been healed, by faith we have the provision we need.

If we choose to yield to Him, it is there that we mature, it is there we are refined and purified, it is there that our faith grows and our character is built, it is there we learn how to abide in His presence, how to walk with Him moment by moment, day by day. It is there we learn to walk in His perfect will for our lives and it is there where we learn that He has not only relentlessly pursued us, not only rescued and saved us, not only shown us grace and mercy, not only restored us, but it is also there we learn that He can sustain us, every single day of our lives.

It is there that we learn to relentlessly pursue Him!

Tent of Hope

Worship in the Tent

Baptisms outside the Tent

Interior of the Tent

Kari's dedication day

Kari-7 months

Kari-3 years

Lee, Kari & I at Uluru

Kari-6 years

Kari-10 years

6

TURNING POINT -
BUSINESS OR MINSTRY

T he year 2015 was a real turning point for us in ministry. We
had just gone through a really tough time. Lee was still recovering
from his arm injury, and we'd also been left pretty disappointed by
another minister. We were a few years into this journey God had called
us to, when Lee decided tent ministry was all too hard. We still owned
our business at this stage, so we planned to get back into drilling. (A
bit like in John 21 - the disciples went back to fishing when Jesus died
on the cross, even after everything they had seen the Lord do!).

We made a couple of phone calls and within a week we had contracted work for the next couple of months. In those few months of
work, we made over $120,000 and decided to go overseas on a holiday.
We went to America for six weeks and splurged on everything we could
and brought suitcases full of gifts home for the kids and grandkids. On
the flight home, however, we realised that it didn't matter how much
money we made, how many things we bought, how big a house we had.
Nothing could satisfy us more than walking in what God had called us
to. We desperately missed seeing people encountering God at the altar
in our tent. We missed being able to give to others what God had given

to us. We missed the incredible highs. We even missed the lows because it was in those times when we felt crushed, that we pressed in for more of Him and He poured the fresh oil of His anointing over us.

Oftentimes in ministry we make sacrifices that others don't see. There are times when we face challenges when there is no solution other than to trust God, or times when we have to face things in our own life that aren't pleasing to God.

In the natural world, the process of making oil is through crushing - when olives or seeds are crushed, oil is created. In the spirit, the process is the same - as we are tested and tried in the crushing, the oil we need is formed and it is this oil that we need to keep our lamps burning until He comes again! (Matthew 25)

Once we had reached the decision that regardless of what we came up against, we were 100% all in, we put our boots back on and got on with the job!

Instead of getting straight back on the road though, we started ministering on the streets in Brisbane, reaching out to those who were living like we once were. We started a homeless program in Fortitude Valley that grew really quickly. We built up a team and were feeding anywhere from eighty to one hundred and twenty people each week. We were given the use of a building right in the centre of Fortitude Valley and every week people were getting saved, baptised, healed, set free, as well as having their physical needs met. We were seeing the Gospel in action, demonstrating that love looks like something!

During this time there was a young couple who would regularly join us each week. They weren't homeless, but were definitely doing it tough. As we got to know them, they shared that they really wanted to get married but simply couldn't afford a wedding. We discussed their desire with the team and decided to help them by organising and paying for a wedding for them! Over the next few weeks, we did some fundraising and we planned. The girls took the young bride shopping for a wedding dress while the boys got fitted for suits; we got flowers and ordered the cake, and not long afterwards, held a beautiful wedding in the middle of Brisbane, complete with a reception afterwards!

After eighteen months on the streets in Brisbane, we were really feeling the Lord calling us back out on the road but felt responsible for the program we had started with the homeless. One night, while we were in the city, one of our team members felt they had a word from God that they were supposed to step up and take responsibility for the homeless program, which in turn would release us to get out on the road again. We prayed about it with them and over the next few weeks we transitioned out as they took over.

We threw ourselves back into the ministry on the road, although we still had the business and Lee was trying to work occasionally, as well as doing outreaches and crusades.

One night, at a weeklong tent crusade in Mt Gravatt, after working all day and then having to come and minister in the tent that evening before packing it down, God spoke to Lee and said, "What's it going to be - the business or the ministry?"

We have no doubt that God would have blessed whatever we chose but Lee replied, "I could never give up the ministry." We now knew without a shadow of doubt that ministry was where He'd called us to, and what He'd called us to do. For some people, having a business or working in the secular world is what God has planned for them, but it wasn't where He wanted us at that time. So, we started the process of selling up and closing the business.

The safest and most fulfilling place to be, is in the will of God and following His direction for our life.

AWAKENING ORANGE

In 2017 we met an incredible couple who have now become very good friends - Daniel and Chelsea Hagen. We had heard about an event they were planning with Ben Fitzgerald, called Awakening Australia, and really felt the Lord calling us to partner with them without knowing anything about them or ever having met them!

We flew down from Queensland and attended a meeting at the Margaret Court arena in Melbourne, Victoria, where we met Daniel for the first time. Then, a few weeks later, he was in Brisbane, so we arranged to meet for lunch. Over that lunch, we let him know that God had spoken to us and that they had our full support for Awakening Australia. Somehow the subject of Orange came up in the conversation and before we knew it, we were planning the first pre-Awakening event in regional New South Wales.

Throughout 2018, we partnered with Awakening Australia, holding pre-Awakening events in both New South Wales and Queensland in the lead up to a huge stadium event in Melbourne.

The first one, Awakening Orange, was phenomenal. With five different churches actively involved, we held evangelism training, a women's morning tea, a men's breakfast, a youth event, and a pastor's/leader's dinner, all in the first week. The second week, we put up the big tent and had nightly revival outreach meetings and a family fun day. On the final Sunday we held a combined churches Sunday morning service in the tent. Seven churches chose to close their normal morning services to join together in unity and lift up the name of Jesus together! We then finished off the crusade with spontaneous water baptisms! Over the two weeks that we were there, we saw about two hundred and fifty decisions made to follow Jesus, both first time and recommitments - it was phenomenal!

We have since done outreaches like this one in several cities, the most recent being in Toowomba, Queensland at the time of writing this book. Many people encountered God, were saved and baptised, healed and set free, and churches united and worked together to see their city transformed, just as the body of Christ should do!

The word says in Psalm 133 that *"where there is unity, God commands a blessing!"* If we want to see our cities and regions impacted with the Gospel, we will need to lay down our own agendas, stop trying to build our own kingdoms and work together, love one another, and unite! *"By this all will know that you are My disciples, if you have love for one another."* (John 13:35)

CHRIST FOR ALL NATIONS (CFAN)

March 2018.

The next month, after Awakening Orange in 2018, we had the opportunity to attend the CfaN School of Evangelism in Orlando, Florida.

What a life changing week of encounter, equipping and empowering! The CfaN School Of Evangelism is a small, intensive training for those who feel called as evangelists. One hundred and twenty students are invited to attend and are immersed in the presence of God, receiving training and impartation from anointed men of God such as Reinhard Bonke (who has now gone to glory), Daniel Kolenda, Michael Koulianos, Todd White and others.

At the end of the week, the final session was one of prayer, impartation and commissioning. All the speakers were in a room, lined up ready for a "Fire Tunnel" (they made two lines facing each other with a gap, and their arms held up and stretched out towards each other to make a 'tunnel') and we (the students) were instructed to line up and enter through the doorway at the end of a hallway.

Walking down the hallway towards the door that led to the room, Lee and I, unbeknown to each other, had a sense that this was a martyrs walk, that today we were going to die (to ourselves). My heart was beating so hard, I started shaking and tears were rolling down my cheeks before I even got to the doorway, as the tangible presence of God was touching me!

As I walked into the room, Todd White was the second one to lay hands on me and I physically felt thrown backwards by the power of God, but instead of falling, I was pulled through to Daniel Kolenda who put two hands on my head, and he yelled FIRE! I literally felt the fire of God go through my body and I fell to the floor, trembling (where I stayed for the next thirty minutes).

Lee on the other hand, went all the way through the fire tunnel three times!

Attending the CfaN School Of Evangelism was, for us, all about dying to ourselves, laying down our lives totally and completely so that we can wholeheartedly say, "It's no longer I that live, but Christ that lives in me!"

There is nothing else that we are here on this earth for, but to know Him and to make Him known.

We are so thankful for the opportunity to have been trained and equipped and to have received impartation from people who are walking the walk of faith and the calling of God on their lives. Men and women who have paid the price and laid down their own lives.

Jesus spent three years with his disciples, teaching them, praying with them, demonstrating the power and presence of God, and then releasing them to carry the presence of God, to walk in integrity and good character, to train and equip others.

Throughout both the Old and New Testaments are instructions for studying, training, equipping, laying on of hands and commissioning.

In Numbers 8:10, God's people lay their hands on the priests to officially commission them as their representatives before God; in Numbers 27:18, Moses lays hands on Joshua to commission him as the new leader of the nation.

In the New Testament, we see that through the laying on of hands in the Gospels, healing is also released, (Matthew 9:18, Mark 5:23), and the Holy Spirit is given and received (Acts 8:17, Acts 19:6).

In both Acts and in Timothy the Bible speaks of laying hands on those who are set apart to commission them for ministry, (Acts 13:3, 1 Timothy 4:14).

KNOCKED DOWN BUT NOT KNOCKED OUT!

October 2018.

In late 2018, we held an outreach in Chinchilla, Queensland. On the second day we were there, we were doing some evangelism training in the tent before heading out on the streets. It became very windy, clouds were swirling around overhead, and we were all watching their movement in awe.

While we were watching, it started to rain quite heavily and the wind became really strong, so I went to put our little girl Kari in the caravan which was at one end of the tent. I grabbed her hand and started walking towards the caravan, but as we did, the whole of that end of the tent lifted off the ground and started falling towards us. Lee called out for everyone to run out of the tent, so we turned quickly and ran in the opposite direction as the tent poles fell around us and the roof collapsed.

It had started hailing by this stage and we all ran out of the falling tent, through the hail and piled into whatever cars were parked outside. We later heard on the news that the freak storm was described as a mini tornado with wind gusts of up to 140km/hr.

One of our team said, "Tent ministry – it's not for the faint hearted!" Definitely not, it's for the faith-hearted!

As quickly as the storm had started, it finished. We all piled out of the cars into water gushing through the park up to our ankles. The tent was completely down, the roof ripped and torn, poles snapped, chairs and screens broken, and the sound equipment and speakers were sitting in the water and mud.

We had two choices - pack up and go home or push forward and keep going. We were reminded of the Scripture in 2 Corinthians that says, *"Though we experience every kind of pressure, we're not crushed. At times we don't know what to do, but quitting is not an option...God has not forsaken us. We may be knocked down, but we're not knocked out."* (2 Cor 4:8-9 TPT).

So, we chose to keep going!

Within half an hour, the Showground caretakers had offered the main pavilion to us to use, as the tent was useless. We started picking things up out of the water and mud, carrying them over to the pavilion. We set up for the meeting that night, including plugging in all the waterlogged sound equipment, which continued to work for the next few days while we did the outreach in the 'Pavilion of Hope', as we'd renamed it!

We returned home the following week thinking we had lost everything, not knowing that our public liability insurance policy included some cover for damage to the tent and equipment. It was a few days later that we found out we had some general insurance, so we put in a claim and the inspector came to assess the damage.

The Lord kept reminding us of the verse in Genesis 50:20, so we started confessing it: *"But as for you, you meant evil against me; but God meant it for good, in order to bring it about as it is this day, to save many people's lives."*

Within a few weeks, the insurance company had agreed to a payout, and we were given enough money to purchase a brand-new second tent (we bought a huge 15m x 30m clear-span marquee which "just happened" to be on a half-price sale), as well as making repairs to the old tent. We were also given a new sound system that was better than one we had! So now we had doubled our capacity! We had extended our tent pegs, as it says in Isaiah 54:2!

TEST OF PROVISION

In so many ways over the years we have experienced God's amazing provision for us in tough times. The Bible says, *"These things I have spoken to you, that in Me you may have peace. In the world you will have tribulation; but be of good cheer, I have overcome the world."* (John 16:33)

There are many verses that warn us that we will have trials and tribulations, persecution and temptations, difficulties and challenges. Psalm 23 is a beautiful scripture of Gods promises for us, but it says things like "Yea, though I walk through the valley of the shadow of death", and "You prepare a table before me in the presence of my enemies".

"The Lord is my shepherd; I shall not want. He makes me to lie down in green pastures; He leads me beside the still waters. He restores my soul; He leads me in the paths of righteousness For His name's sake. Yea, though I walk through the valley of the shadow of death, I will fear no evil; For You are with me; Your rod and Your staff, they comfort me. You prepare a table before me in

the presence of my enemies; You anoint my head with oil; My cup runs over. Surely goodness and mercy shall follow me All the days of my life; And I will dwell in the house of the Lord Forever." (Psalms 23)

God has never promised that once we surrender our lives to Him and choose to live the way He intended and planned for us, that life would be all sunshine and lollipops! He never said we wouldn't go through difficulties or come under attack in some way.

In fact, He says quite clearly that we will face trials and tribulations, that we will experience death and enemy attacks. BUT He has also promised that He is always with us. He has promised comfort, He has promised restoration, and He has promised His goodness and mercy!

As the body of Christ, we are a family, working together in unity and everyone plays their part. But we are also an army! We need to be trained, armed, ready for battle.

When trials, temptations, persecution, or whatever else comes our way, we know that they are opportunities to grow in character, to grow in strength, to grow spiritually, to learn to trust our father, and to learn to withstand the challenges and pressures that the enemy sends to distract us from the path of life.

One thing we have learnt over the years is the test of provision, and that God alone is our Provider. Although sometimes He uses people, we cannot rely on people, they are not our source or our supply. The Bible says, *"He will supply all our needs according to His riches in glory in Christ Jesus."* (Philippians 4:19)

There have often been times when we were waiting on finances and the Lord will come through right at the last minute! Sometimes we are tempted to help Him and look for ways ourselves.

One story that comes to mind was just before a major outreach in New South Wales. Finances were pretty tight, and someone offered to fill both our trucks with diesel. We knew, however, that technically the fuel wasn't theirs to give as they were using a fuel card owned by a company that they worked for. Overlooking the facts though, we reasoned that this was a "blessing", when in fact it was actually receiving an unrighteous offering.

About an hour into the ten-hour drive, the bigger truck started playing up, so we pulled over and realised that diesel had been leaking out. There was a pinhole in the fuel filter! About ten minutes later the smaller truck did exactly the same thing and had the same problem - a pinhole in its fuel filter. God was obviously trying to tell us something. We slowly got both trucks to the next town by which time most of the diesel had leaked out, so we drained the rest, replaced the fuel filters, refilled the tanks, and repented! The trucks were fine for the rest of the trip, we had an incredible outreach with people saved, healed and set free; and the Lord provided everything we needed, with surplus finances at the end. Lesson learnt!

SCHOOL OF AWAKENING

2019.

In 2019, we had the opportunity to attend the Awakening Europe, School of Awakening, in Germany.

Although we were already in ministry with tent outreaches etc., this school set us on fire and launched us into the next season. After 'dying' at CfaN, we were 'awakened' in Lorrach, Germany!!

We both had powerful encounters with God every day and learnt so many practical ministry tools that have equipped us to walk exactly where He asks us!

During 2019 we also spent time studying and completed our Certificate IV in Ministry, even though we had already been in ministry for about eight years! The Bible says in 2 Timothy 2:15 to *"study to show yourself approved...rightly dividing the word of truth."*

There is always more to learn in the Word, always more ways to grow. The Christian walk is a journey and growth is vital for that journey. We weren't made to be stagnant; we should be growing in holiness, growing in wisdom and knowledge, growing in grace, maturing and being transformed into the likeness of Jesus. It says in 2 Peter 3:18 to *"grow in the grace and knowledge of our Lord and Saviour Jesus Christ."*

HARVEST NOW

2020.

I can't write this book without mentioning another of our very dear friends, Daz Chettle. Daz lives in New Zealand with his beautiful wife Briana and their children. We met in 2017 after we had heard him preaching online and had booked him to come and minister in the tent! At our very first meeting, Lee and Daz had an instant connection because of their passion for souls. We were sitting in a restaurant somewhere in Melbourne and the two of them ended up weeping over lunch as they shared their hearts and God's heart for His children to come home.

At the beginning of 2020, Daz launched Harvest Now School of Evangelism, in Christchurch, New Zealand and invited us to go over. We had already done a fair bit of ministry together, had attended CfaN together and we couldn't wait to join him for his very first SOE.

It was such a powerful week of ministry and training; we were equipped and challenged to press in for more, to run harder, to seek God's heart for the lost even more! These schools are incredible for equipping Christians to GO!

Evangelist Andrew Cannon (another amazing friend and champion for the Kingdom), and Daz are the directors of Harvest NOW and these schools have now been held in the UK and the USA as well as in New Zealand. If you're feeling called as an evangelist, I would encourage you to check out the Harvest Now School of Evangelism!

COVID-19

March 2020.

While we were in New Zealand, the COVID pandemic was brewing, and just before we were due to return to Australia, lockdowns were starting. We caught the last flight back into the country, full of the Holy Spirit, ON FIRE and ready to bring in the harvest. But had to go straight into quarantine for two weeks!

We immediately started praying and asking the Lord for ways to reach and connect with people while in lockdown. At the time we were renovating one house and just about to build another one, so during the next few months we had people coming to us - various tradesmen and delivery drivers; I did nearly all my shopping online so had plenty of people delivering groceries and other items to our door and we even had someone break down outside the front of our house! And every single person heard the Gospel.

We called some of our team and met with them to plan different ways we could get back out into the community. One thing that was severely lacking was providing food for the homeless. Although some were temporarily housed in motels, most of the charities that provided meals had closed down. As this was something we had done before, we could certainly do it again, so we did. When no one was allowed outside of their homes because of various restrictions, by providing this emergency service we could still get out on the streets! While lockdowns were being strictly enforced, I would cook meals and individually package them and Lee would drive into town to deliver them, with one of our team members. This outreach continued throughout Covid-19 and, at the time of writing this book, has been going for over three years. There is now a regular barbeque in Brisbane city every Monday night where our team provides food, toiletries, sleeping bags and other essential items for around 200 people, and it is continuing to grow.

There are ALWAYS opportunities to share the Gospel, whether it be to your neighbour, a stranger, work colleague, family, or friends. We just need to be looking for wherever God opens the door and provides the opportunity!

"Make the most of every opportunity in these evil days. Don't act thoughtlessly but understand what the Lord wants you to do." (Ephesians 5:16)

"Pray that I will proclaim this message as clearly as I should. Live wisely among those who are not believers and make the most of every opportunity.

Let your conversation be gracious and attractive so that you will have the right response for everyone." (Colossians 4:4-6)

CfaN Orlando School of Evangelism

Todd White, Lee & I (& Tom)

Daniel Kolenda, Lee & I

School of Awakening

Snow-Lorrach, Germany for SOA

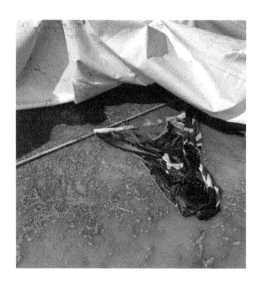

Chinchilla Tent Collapse

Knocked down but not knocked out!!

Street Outreach

7

MINISTRY EXPANDS – YES TO MORE

EMPOWERED EVENTS

D ecember 2020.

After so many lockdowns throughout 2020 with churches closing, no corporate gatherings, constrained worship meetings, towards the end of the year we were so keen to break out of the restrictions!

We also noticed during the COVID-19 season just how much "the Church" needed equipping from the evangelist. In our passion and desire to see souls saved, we (along with many others who are called as evangelists), had forgotten what our job was. Along with apostles, pastors, teachers and prophets, we are called to equip the saints for the work of the ministry.

And so, the idea of Empowered School of Evangelism and Activation was birthed. Our first one was held in December 2020 - a four-day intensive school for those feeling called as evangelists. It was such a powerful time of equipping and activating, extended worship and seeking the heart of God, people returning to their first love, breaking off fear of man, practical training and sending people out into the harvest field.

We were so blown away by the hunger of the people that came from all over Australia, and by the way the Lord poured out His Spirit, that before the final day had ended, we had already decided to hold another school!

At the time of writing, we have now held seven schools. Many ministries have been birthed and multiple outreaches have been started through these schools. During the fifth school we felt such a shift - the Lord was speaking to us about expanding and stretching us even further. We then received prophetic words about Empowered becoming an apostolic hub which confirmed exactly what God had been speaking to us. We were seeing not just evangelists being trained and sent out, but people stepping into their calling of pastor and planting churches, as well as prophetic voices starting to exercise their gift. So, we changed the name to Empowered IN HIM Apostolic School of Activation. We opened it up to those feeling called to all areas of the fivefold ministry of the Body and Christ (apostles, pastors, teachers, prophets and evangelists).

TESTIMONIES FROM EMPOWERED

Brydon: *I went to the Easter 2021 Empowered Evangelism conference on the Sunshine Coast. Prior to going I had always struggled with breakthrough from the fear of man. Throughout the conference I witnessed God move powerfully in people's lives. Not only that, I also saw the passion and desire in the ministers to see the Gospel preached boldly by every believer. During the activations I was able to step out and share the love of Jesus with people and pray for strangers.*

When I got home, I went out every day for the first week to share Jesus on the streets and to stay activated in the things I had learnt. I ended up taking my kids out and they also got to experience evangelism for themselves.

Since the school I have seen heaps of people healed, born again and receive the seed of the gospel on the streets. I have also been able to lead outreach groups of people who have never stepped out before also.

Bianca: *I was raised in a Christian home with parents in ministry. I had also been ministering but had never led anyone to the Lord outside of church. During the activation/outreach, I was able to lead four young men to the Lord out on the streets!*

**Both Brydon and Bianca are now pastoring incredible churches on the Gold Coast, and in Rockhampton, Queensland. They are seeing God move powerfully not just in the church, but also outside the four walls of the church, in everyday life, and are training and raising up others to "Go into all the world!"

Shar: *I attended the very first Empowered and was massively impacted. Over the four days, we were immersed in the presence of God through the worship, challenged and equipped through the teaching and powerfully ministered to on the altar. As the fivefold ministers were speaking, it was like every word was piercing my heart. The mantle these guys are carrying to empower us, equip us and to send us out was so tangible. I was so radically touched, the school was a launchpad for the coming months once we returned to our home in Perth, Western Australia.*

John and Kylie Kirkegaard: *We have been so blessed to be able to attend the Empowered Conference three times over the last two years and each one has undoubtedly left its mark. Lee and Peta facilitate such an incredible opportunity for the Holy Spirit to do what only He can do.*

All three occasions were incredible, but the one held in 2021 in Toowoomba was particularly life changing for our family. We were in a bit of limbo with our direction. Career versus ministry seemed to be on our hearts as John, my husband, was studying at the time.

On this particular day of the conference, I felt such a burden in my heart, like we had hit the ceiling and didn't know how to break through. As I was helping the kids into the car, Lee was talking with our friends. Before I knew it, I was being ushered over as a word was being given to John. The word was clear, that there would come a time to choose between ministry or the career he was studying towards. Lee said that God would bless either one, but we would need to choose at some point. He shared that he had thought John was a Pastor and was surprised to learn he was not.

John and I have absolute respect for the prophetic, however we have seen it abused many times, so we are not ones to jump at a word from someone, especially if we do not know them well. We took it with a grain of salt.

No more than three hours later, John received a phone call. He was offered the job of a lifetime that would get him exactly where he had originally planned to go with his studies. What convenient timing! The moment I heard what was going on I prayed he would not take it. I knew it was the carrot being dangled and that God had something else. He hung up the phone and after moments of back-and-forth conversation it hit him. The word spoken over him three hours prior.

He turned down the job a few days later and by the next week he was offered a Family Pastor position at a church in Toowoomba. We are now heading to America to further our study of the Word, in Florida and we have seen God open every single door for our family. Safe to say, we are so glad we chose ministry!

We are so, so grateful for these conferences and for what Lee and Peta do for the body of Christ. It is such a blessing, and we know that what they facilitate, allows the Holy Spirit to move and propel you where He wants you to be.

Samantha: My testimony is of financial blessing. I attended the Empowered school after receiving a free ticket and was also blessed with accommodation. Whilst at the school, there was an offering taken up to cover costs and even though I couldn't really afford it, I felt to sow my last $20. On the outreach that afternoon I was feeling down and regretting sowing the money. I was sitting on a bench instead of doing any sort of evangelism or outreach and stranger came up to me and said they felt to give me $20!

Back at the evening session in the school, I was sharing this testimony and, when I had finished and was back in my seat, people in the school started coming up & dropping money in my lap...at the end of the evening, I had over $700 and was completely overwhelmed with the goodness of God.

MIRACLES AND TESTIMONIES

Testimonies are such a powerful thing! One of my favourite verses in the Bible is in Revelation and it says, *"And they overcame and conquered him (the enemy, the devil) because of the blood of the Lamb and because of the word of their testimony, for they did not love their life and renounce their faith even when faced with death."* (Revelation 12:11)

Sharing our testimony is a mighty weapon against the enemy.

The word testimony in Hebrew is *'Aydooth'* which means *'do it again with the same power and authority'*. Every time we speak out, or read a testimony we are saying Lord, 'do it again' with the same power and authority.

When we are sharing the Gospel in our everyday life with those around us, it is most effective to share a personal testimony, to share what God has done for you in your life. People can debate and argue different theologies, but no one can argue with your own personal testimony.

We have seen God move so powerfully throughout the years as we have stepped out into the things He asked of us. There have been countless first-time salvations and prodigals returning, physical healings and miracles and people delivered and set free from addiction and demonic oppression.

These are just a few of those testimonies. I pray that as you read these stories, God will do it again, with the same power and authority.

Ryan: In December 2011 we were in Port Macquarie, the fifth city on our first twelve-week tour. The tent was set up right next to Town Beach; it was a beautiful spot. It was also a very popular spot with constant traffic driving into the car park, right past the tent.

During one of the night meetings, Lee and one of the team members, Jeremy, got a couple of chairs and sat outside the tent so that they could share the Gospel with those who didn't make it into the tent but were driving through the car park.

They had the opportunity to pray for so many people that night, including one guy who was suicidal. Four years later, we got the following message from Jeremy:

> "So ...I answered my door to a young man this afternoon who was from Wollongong. He was working for the Smith Family raising money, and he asked what I did for work.
>
> I told him I was a chaplain and he exclaimed "Wow. I've always wanted to do that work."
>
> I let him know it was fun and asked what his faith journey had been like. He told me that his name was Ryan, and he was from Port Macquarie. He said he found Christ about four years ago at a tent called the Tent of Hope which had been set up for ministry. He said he came one night and spoke to an older guy and a bigger young guy in the carpark outside the tent, while he was depressed and contemplating life. He said he was blown away that the older white-haired guy went to get a couple of chairs and they both sat with him and talked about life while they shared the Gospel. Three days later he walked into the tent and gave his heart to Christ at the altar call.
>
> I asked him if he drove a little red Mazda 323 and he said "yes" and gave me a funny look. Then I told him that I was the young, bigger guy, and the older guy was Lee Taberner who owned the tent. He was blown away as we shared stories about that week. I was blown away that God walked him into an incredible journey that he is still on, and that God led him to my door while he was visiting town!"

Adam: One testimony of deliverance we will never forget was that of Adam at a tent crusade on the North side of Brisbane. Adam was heavily into drugs, tortured by demonic sprits and had been walking past the tent and felt drawn to come in even though there was no meeting on at the time. But he wasn't able to walk inside. He tried several times but felt something stopping him every time. He was desperate to find help and ended up sending an email to the website that was on our sign at the front of the tent. This is the email he sent:

"I walked into that tent, it was almost empty just a couple people I felt God's hand and I ran out I think I have some evil in me that don't want me there. I tried. I will try again. I need God back!!! Funny cause the tents across the road from Me!!"

Not knowing who this young man was, our team prayed, and the following night he walked into the tent whilst the meeting was on and when the altar call was given, he made his way up to the front. As he was receiving prayer, the demonic spirits in him manifested and he tried to run out of the tent, but Lee and some of the other guys physically stopped him and continued to pray. Adam received such a powerful deliverance; at one stage his tongue came out like a snake as the demons tried to resist, but they had to leave at the name of Jesus!

After this encounter with God, we kept in touch with Adam and journeyed with him as he continued his walk with the Lord. Adam went through Bible College, met and married a wonderful lady and they have two beautiful children. Adam is now a Christian rap artist and he and his family continue to serve the Lord.

David: David was brought by friends to our tent on the very first tour we did. He was at rock bottom and had planned to end his life that night. Instead, he had such a radical encounter with God, was instantly delivered and set free! He played the saxophone and later that same week joined in with the worship band. He later went on to play with a very well-known guitarist and now travels throughout Australia, performing.

Lymes disease: Mandy came to one of our tent meetings in New South Wales, severely debilitated with Lymes disease. She couldn't walk properly, couldn't speak properly, and had very little control of body movements. As we began praying for her, she began to see in the Spirit. She saw numerous demons that were attached to her body. As she pointed them out, we rebuked them and told them to leave her body.

It was a long process as she lay on the grass in the tent while we prayed for her for about an hour. When we all felt the peace of God, we helped Mandy up and she was completely healed! She was totally delivered - she could walk, talk and had total control of her body!

Stage 4 cancer: We had the tent set up in the Mt Gravatt Showground in 2014 when Lois attended one of the meetings. Lois had stage 4 cancer, had lost her hair, and was wearing a wig. At the end of the meeting, she came to receive prayer but before anyone was even near her, God touched her. She was forcefully pushed back through four rows of chairs and laid out on the ground. Lee went to help her up however she insisted God was healing her. We didn't see her leave the tent that night but a few weeks later I ran into her in Koorong, and she let me know that she was completely healed - no sign of cancer in her body. Lois has since written a book about her healing.

Deafness healed: We have seen a number of people healed from deafness, one being a young girl who was completely deaf in one ear. She was totally healed, instantly. Her dad, John, testified later they'd had her hearing checked and the healing verified by the doctors.

As well as our own amazing testimonies over the past few years and those of people we have ministered to who have experienced the goodness of God, miraculous power, provision and more, our team members have also been impacted by the ways God moves while travelling with us. Here is one of those testimonies from Luke Wilson.

There are many testimonies that Luke can share, but one that stands out would be a trip that he and Lee took in 2021. They had to drive the big truck down to Melbourne and back to help some friends who were moving up to Queensland.

On the trip back to Queensland they stopped at the Moree hot pools for a break. The two of them hopped into the hot pools before they rested for the night. The pools were quite full and as they always do, Lee and Luke both started sharing the Gospel to a full pool of strangers! Some jumped out, some listened, but one guy in the pool was so responsive and ready that they ended up leading him to Jesus in the pool; they, then asked if he wanted to be baptised (since they were in the water anyway!), to which he said "yes!". So, in a pool full of people, they baptised this guy and when he came up out of the water he was staring at them with wide eyes and exclaimed, "Wow, there is a guy with a big white beard standing behind you both with one hand on each of your shoulders, smiling!"

What an encounter!!

FIRST NATION COMMUNITIES

2021.

In 2021, we were invited up to Cape York in Far North Queensland, to minister in several First Nation communities. Although we had worked with Aboriginal people previously and, in fact, have many First Nation friends, we had never been to a closed Aboriginal community.

We took a small team and drove for five days to get up there, three of those days on corrugated dirt roads.

As soon as we arrived, we absolutely fell in love. The beautiful people in these communities were so open to the Gospel. We took jumping castles for the children, and fairy floss, popcorn and snow cones, plenty of games and we even created skits. The children were gorgeous and had so much fun, as did we all, while showing the love of Christ and sharing the Gospel. In Aurukun, we had a lady healed of deafness, another lady was blind and received her sight! There were many decisions made for Christ among both the adults and children. We were able to minister in the local churches where many had never experienced the power of the Holy Spirit prior to us coming. It was beautiful to see how they opened their hearts to the Lord and to watch Him move amongst them.

The only regret from that trip was that we didn't stay long enough; both the team and the locals cried when we left. We can't wait to go back!

While in Rockhampton on a ministry trip, we were doing some

street outreach and met Kevin, an older Aboriginal man. He was at the river with a bunch of other First Nation people, most of whom were drunk (including Kevin!).

A few weeks previously, I had been given a copy of the book *God's Dreaming* (a book of Aboriginal paintings representing the Bible). Remembering that I had it in the car, I went to get it to show Kevin. This book impacted him so much that he began explaining the pictures and telling the Bible stories to us!

After spending the next few days with our team, Kevin made a decision to give his life to Jesus. He then returned to his community, Woorabinda, to make a fresh start. He connected with the local pastor who knew Kevin previously. She saw such a change in him that she contacted us and invited us to bring a team to the community.

We went in early June 2022 and God moved powerfully through the children in the community. We saw around one hundred decisions made for Jesus and baptised over forty children! We have continued to make regular trips to Woorabinda as God started to move through this community.

On our most recent trip to Woorabinda, we took a large team with us and painted the outside of the local church as well as running children's programs every afternoon and revival meetings each evening. We had such an outpouring of the Holy Spirit that people, hearing the meetings from their backyards on the opposite side of town, drove over to us and responded to the altar call.

That Sunday, the local church was inundated with new people and the pastor decided to start midweek home group meetings and a youth group!

PIONEERING

From the start of God calling us into ministry we knew that He was asking us to pioneer - to breakthrough and take ground for Him, to push through any obstacles, to smash down any walls, to keep going no matter what we come up against, like a bulldozer, flattening anything that stands in our way.

As you have heard, sometimes the road has been rough, the battles long and hard and there have been tears and heartache along the way. But we have continued to give Him our 'yes', trusting that His way is better. There have also been joyous victories, celebrations, visions and dreams fulfilled that far outweigh all the challenges. We aren't promised smooth sailing, but we are promised He will be with us in every storm. When we give God our 'yes', we are enlisting in His army, we are signing up for war, but we know we are on the winning side and there is nothing more fulfilling than walking in the path that God planned for you.

In the beginning of 2022, we felt the Lord asking us to stretch even further. We had been in full time, itinerant ministry for several years and although we love travelling around, seeing the Lord touch lives all across our nation, we knew He was asking more of us - to train, equip, raise up and send out other soldiers. The Bible says that "the harvest is ripe, but the labourers are few" (Matthew 9:37). There are over seven billion people on this planet, and we definitely can't witness to, save, pastor and teach them all by ourselves. The Kingdom army that is needed is huge. If we are to see revival across the world, we need to be multiplying. The army of God needs to be expanding.

And so, we began another journey as we felt the Lord leading us to plant a church. To build an apostolic hub; a place where people can come and encounter God, where the Holy Spirit can move freely without restraint. A place to be discipled, equipped, fortified, activated, and sent back out into the harvest field.

This too was a process for us as we again laid down our own ideas and agendas, submitted ourselves again to His will for our lives and followed His footsteps. The Lord had brought another beautiful family into our lives, quite divinely, around the same time as He started speaking to us about this, and so the journey began with Alex and Krystal Fe'ao – together we were going to plant a church!

Finally on June 28th of 2023, we held our very first meeting in Woodridge, Queensland, with around 70 people, and Fire Church Brisbane South began to be birthed!

Even though we have been in itinerant ministry for over 10 years (at the time of writing), we believe wholeheartedly in the importance of the local church, of being planted and having the covering and support of your pastors and leaders. The Bible says in Psalm 92 that those who are planted in the house of the Lord will flourish; as their roots go deep, they will bear much fruit! Having a church family to grow with, to learn with and to build with is so important for our spiritual journey.

Being planted in God's house gives us the right environment and opportunities to be discipled and to disciple others, to develop our gifts and callings, to grow in obedience and humility, to overcome offence and to keep ourselves accountable. If you are planted in the house of God, you will be active, engaged and committed which will lead to you flourishing and bearing much fruit!

Chelsea & I with our children

Daniel, Lee, Brydon (+ kids)

Lee, Daniel Hagen & myself

Phil & Julie Oldfield, Lee & I

Lee, myself, Terry & Sue Moore

Lee, Daz Chettle & I

Mum, Lee, Daz & I

Carmen Lye, myself, Briana Chettle, Daz, Lee & Michael Lye

Andrew Cannon, Lee & I

Lee, Tim Hall & I

New Tent

Empowered IN HIM training schools

Ministering together

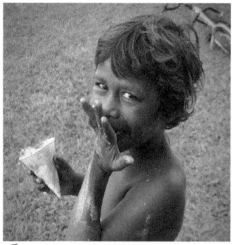

Gorgeous little faces...

Snow Cones!

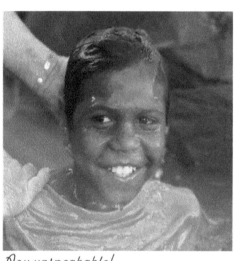

Joy unspeakable!

Baptisms in the back of the ute

So precious

Kari & Zoe in Aurukun

First Nation Communities

Pioneering-Fire Church Brisbane South

Family

8

RELENTLESS PURSUIT

Throughout this book, I have written about how God has relentlessly pursued us. Even when we were running in the opposite direction, His love chased us down. His desire was always for us to encounter Himself and to remain in an intimate relationship with Him.

Imagine being married but never looking at your husband or wife, not talking to them, not being intimate with them and not spending time together. And yet this is so often what we're like with God.

As I mentioned earlier, there was a time early on in our journey when, far too often, Lee and I woke up each day and didn't even acknowledge His presence. We went about our day making decisions without even a thought of His plans or purposes for us. We didn't look to Him. We didn't talk to Him.

This may be how you are living right now, but He wants to encounter YOU!

At some point along our journey, the pursuit started to work both ways - Him pursuing us and now us pursuing Him. A relationship works both ways and there is always more of Him that we can receive - He is our source of life, our daily bread, the air we breathe.

I heard this quote recently:

> *Yesterday's pursuit does not qualify you for today's relationship.*
> Cherise Marler

Pursuing Christ is not a one-off thing, it is a daily decision. We can't stop pursuing Him. We must remain in the place of intimacy, continually seeking His face. The highest calling we have is to seek Him.

"When "you said, "Seek My face," My heart said to You, "Your face, Lord, I will seek."" (Psalm 7:8)

Our relationship with our Creator truly is a relentless pursuit as there is always more to be pressing in for. We need to keep our lamps filled with oil, keep the passion for Him alive in our hearts, keep the fire burning in our lives, because the alternative is becoming lukewarm, complacent, apathetic, indifferent.

There is a song I love called "Nothing Else"; the lyrics of the song say, *"Nothing else will do, I just want You".*

Is this true? Do we really want Jesus more than anything? How often do we become distracted by day-to-day stuff, by the things of this world? By our jobs? Even by ministry?

If we could see and understand just how short our time here on earth really is, in comparison to all of eternity, would we live differently? The Bible says we are aliens, just passing through (1 Chronicles 29:15). We are not of this world, our home is in Heaven, but our time here is so very important.

All our days on earth are written in His book, every intricate detail of our lives. Are we living out what He has written? Or are we writing our own pages? Don't waste the time you have been given. Some of us may be at the beginning of the book, some halfway through, some may be on the very last page. We must make every moment count. One day very soon, we will all have to give an account to God of what we did with what He gave us.

My constant prayer is that I would not become distracted, not look to the right, or left, but keep my eyes fixed on Him alone, my eyes locked on His eyes, daily pursuing Him, daily laying down my life, daily seeking His face, daily surrendering my thoughts and fixing my mind on Him alone.

The more we press in, the closer He comes. God responds to hunger; the more we hunger and thirst after God, the more He will pour Himself out on us. The Bible says to draw near to God and He will draw near to us, (James 4:8). As we become consumed by His love for us, hearing His heartbeat, His desires become ours, just like dancers dancing gracefully together, moving together as one.

There are two birds mentioned in the Bible and both demonstrate fixing our eyes on Christ - the dove and the eagle.

Song of Solomon talks about the dove's eyes. The interesting thing about doves is that they have binocular vision, which means that they can only focus on one thing at a time, which is usually their mate. When they look at their mate, they aren't distracted by anything, their gaze is fixed on the one thing that matters. Doves have been nicknamed 'love birds'. If you watch a pair of doves, you'll notice they are always watching each other, always doing what the other one does.

I read recently that eagles have an extra membrane over their eyes that other birds don't have which allows them to look directly at the sun without damaging their vision. The eagle uses this advantage as protection from his enemy, the condor, which is the largest bird in the world. When the eagle is attacked by the condor, it will fly directly into the sun and the condor cannot see to follow him. We can learn something from this - stay focused on the Son!

We hear of different places in the world where God has manifested His presence and remained. Thousands of people have travelled from all over to meet with Him in these places, where cities were shaken, where crime rates dropped, where the pubs and nightclubs closed because everyone was at church, where meetings went on for hours upon hours as the Spirit of God was poured out. Some of us may have experienced this or even had just a small taste of it. Why does this happen in these places? Because the people want Him - they are hungry for His presence. They want Him more than what is on TV, they want Him more than whatever this world is offering, they want Him more than anything and they are willing to pay the price; willing to lay down their sin, willing to lay down their distractions, willing to lay down their convenience, willing to lay down their lives.

When we take our eyes off Jesus however, and start looking at the things around us, the flow of His power subsides, the pressure of the enemy returns, the temptations of life try to pull us away and even the distractions of ministry can turn our eyes from the King. When our gaze is only on His blazing eyes of fire, we find all that we need. His love burns away the dross, His burning eyes of fire refine and purify us. He is our protection and our joy.

He is the One we adore, our deliverer, our hearts desire - Jesus, the King of Glory!

CHALLENGE

The heart of God is for His creation, those created in His image, His sons and daughters, and His desire is for all to know Him.

As we remain in that intimate place with Jesus, we learn to feel His heart, His passion for the lost. Because it is only as we go deeper, as we abide in Him and He in us, that we can grow and bear fruit.

"Go into all the world", is the great commission in Matthew 26:19, but how many of us are actually fulfilling it? It's not just the job of the evangelists to fulfil this commission, it is the job of every single Christian. We are all called to be His witnesses. We are all called to carry His presence. We were all created in God's image, for His glory, to know Him and to make Him known!

In Matthew 4:19 Jesus says, *"Follow me and I will make you fishers of men"*. Is it possible to truly follow Christ without fishing for men, without sharing the gospel and without compelling people to come to Jesus?

When Jesus spoke these words to Peter and Andrew, they immediately dropped their nets and followed Him. They left their livelihoods, everything they had known, to fulfil His call on their lives.

In Ezekiel 3:10-11 it says, *"Then he added, "Son of man, let all my words sink deep into your own heart first. Listen to them carefully for yourself. Then go to your people in exile and say to them, 'This is what the Sovereign Lord says!' Do this whether they listen to you or not.""*

In Mark 4:26-29 Jesus tells us the parable of the Sower. One thing to notice is that the farmer sowed the seed. He didn't pray about sowing it, he didn't wait for the perfect opportunity, he didn't get someone more qualified to do it, he just did it! Jesus says the harvest is ripe, but we definitely will not see that harvest if we aren't sowing seeds.

In this parable the farmer scattered the seed everywhere. Some fell on rocky ground, some on thorny ground and some on good, fertile ground. Because of God's extravagant love for mankind, He wants everyone to have the opportunity to know Him. It is not up to us to decide who is ready to hear the Gospel and who isn't, just scatter seeds everywhere - the power is in the seed! The Bible says that His Word will not return to Him void but will accomplish that which it was sent to do.

If you've spent any time at all reading the Bible, you would have noticed that the majority of the people who followed God pursued Him relentlessly. They didn't just casually follow Him, they followed Him with reckless abandon. They gave up everything they had and followed Him with a tireless passion and their lives were turned upside down because of this passion. They gave up everything they knew and left it all behind, burning the bridges to their old lives, to be who God had called them to be and to do what He had called them to do.

We're not called to be Sunday Christians; we need to be ALL IN!

So often, as time passes and we've been walking with God for some time, spiritual apathy can start to creep in, or in other words, complacency or lukewarmness.

Revelation 3:15-16 says, *"I know your works, that you are neither cold* nor hot. I could wish you were cold or hot. So then, because you are lukewarm, and neither cold nor hot, I will vomit you out of My mouth."

Then verse 19 says "As many as I love, I rebuke and chasten. Therefore, be ZEALOUS and repent."

Zealous means enthusiastic and eager, ardently active, devoted and diligent, intense, marked by fervent passion. The opposite of zealous is apathetic, complacent, dispassionate, indifferent and unconcerned.

> The pursuit of God is not a part-time, weekend exercise. If it is, chances are you will experience a part-time, weekend free-dom. Abiding requires a kind of staying power. The pursuit is relentless. It hungers and thirsts. It pants as the deer after the mountain brook. It takes the kingdom by storm...The pursuit of God is a pursuit of passion. Indifference will not do. To abide in the Word is to hang on tenaciously. A weak grip will soon slip away. Discipleship requires staying power. We sign up for duration. We do not graduate until heaven.
>
> R.C. Sproul

So how do we stay in that place of passion?

- **Remain in that first love** - "Nevertheless, I have this against you, that you have left your first love. Remember therefore from where you have fallen; repent and do the first works, or else I will come to you quickly and remove your lampstand from its place—unless you repent." (Revelation 2:4-5 NKJV)
  Everyone remembers that first encounter, that first love - you just have to tell somebody! You can't keep it to yourself!
  Psalm 51:12-13 says, "Restore to me the joy of Your salvation, And uphold me by Your generous Spirit. Then I will teach transgressors Your ways, And sinners shall be converted to You."

If you have truly encountered God, you can't contain the love that He pours into you, you can't contain the joy that bubbles up from your belly, you have a river of life within you that has to be let out!

Stay in that intimate place with Jesus, spend time with Him daily, spend time in the Word, daily, be in constant communion with Him.

- **Abide in Him** - Abiding isn't just kicking back and soaking. Abiding is actually being obedient, submitting to the Word. To abide in Christ means so much more than we think. To 'abide' or 'dwell' means to make our home IN HIM. To be fully settled, not just a temporary visit on Sundays or mid-week meetings, but to permanently live in constant communion with our Saviour. To allow His Word to fill our minds, direct our will and transform our affections. It is a relationship of intimacy, in the secret place. Not only does the Word talk about us abiding in Him, but also Him abiding in us; God Himself makes His home in us. He is the vine and we are the branches. This dwelling place isn't a dead, lifeless home, it is alive and growing. It is bearing fruit and reproducing! As we grow more in Christ, He grows stronger in us and we will walk as He walked, we will talk as He talked; His very Presence in us will change the atmosphere wherever we go. The story of Paul and Silas is an example of this. In Acts 16 we are told the story of how they were imprisoned for preaching the Gospel and casting an evil spirit out of a young girl. While they were in prison though, they began to sing and worship the Lord, and as they did, the atmosphere around them changed. The place began to shake, and the prison doors flung open - not just theirs, but everyone who was in the prison! Their lives, sold out for Jesus, had an effect on every person in that place. In the same way our lives sold out for Him, should affect those around us.

- **Stay on fire** - Leviticus 6 talks about sacrifices and in verses 8-13 gives instructions for burnt offerings and it mentions three times in those few verses that the fire must never go out!

Romans 12 says that now WE are the living sacrifices, *"I beseech you therefore, brethren, by the mercies of God, that you present your bodies a living sacrifice, holy, acceptable to God, which is your reasonable service."* (Romans 12:1)

We need to keep the fire burning in our lives.

"I'm writing to encourage you to fan into a flame and rekindle the fire of the spiritual gift God imparted to you when I laid my hands upon you." (2 Timothy 1:6 TPT)

- **Don't get comfortable** - We aren't called to be comfortable, in fact Jesus promised He would send 'The Comforter'. When we get comfortable, we stop growing; when we get comfortable, we become complacent.

There is a generation right now that is searching for the truth, and we have the answer - His name is Jesus!

FINISHING WELL

"Well done good and faithful servant" are the words we all long to hear on the day we enter into Glory! This is the end goal of the journey we are on, to arrive in the very throne room of God, to see Him Face to face and hear Him say "well done".

"Therefore we also, since we are surrounded by so great a cloud of witnesses, let us lay aside every weight, and the sin which so easily ensnares us, and let us run with endurance the race that is set before us, looking unto Jesus, the author and finisher of our faith, who for the joy that was set before Him endured the cross, despising the shame, and has sat down at the right hand of the throne of God." ((Hebrews 12:1-2 NKJV)

We are "the joy set before Him", our lives living to honour Him are His joy. He endured a torture like we will never know, to pay the price for our very lives.

He is so worthy of all our worship, all our affection, all our devotion.

The lyrics of a song by Jeremy , *We Crown You*, are my heart's cry to Him:

To the One
Who wore a crown of thorns
To the One
Who took the lash and scourge
For the hands and feet that were pierced by nails
For the sacrifice that has torn the veil
We crown You!
We fall face down and we worship!
We all cry out "You are worthy God!"
"You are worthy, God!"
We crown You!
We fall face down and we worship!
We all cry out "You are worthy God!"
"You are worthy, God!"
To the One who gave His very life away
Who took upon Himself all our guilt and shame
Hanging on a cross
For the world He loved
With His precious blood
Purchased men for God
We crown You!
We fall face down and we worship!
We all cry out "You are worthy God!"
"You are worthy, God!"
We crown You!
We fall face down and we worship!
We all cry out "You are worthy God!"
"You are worthy, God!"
To the One Who endured all the shame of the cross
To the Lamb Who was slain as atonement for us

To the Son Who overcame all the power of death
We praise...
For the stripes, for the wounds
For the beating You bore
For the tears, for the blood
That was willingly poured
For the merciful, wonderful, majesty of Your love!
We crown You!
We fall face down and we worship!
We all cry out "You are worthy God!"
"You are worthy, God!"
We crown You!
We fall face down and we worship!
We all cry out "You are worthy God!"
"You are worthy, Lord!"
(Jeremy Riddle, Lindy Carol Conaut, Tayla Rede. Capital CMG
Publishing)

Whatever we are doing in life, whatever our gifts and callings may be, what is important to God is not what we do for Him but how we minister to Him when we come in from the fields.

Don't look for praise from man. The disciples were never commended by Jesus for performing miracles. We shouldn't expect a reward for doing as Christ commanded, however, of Mary's extravagant worship He said, *"Assuredly, I say to you, wherever this gospel is preached in the whole world, what this woman has done will also be told as a memorial to her."* (Matthew 26:13)

When Jesus came to their house, Martha was busy making sure everything was just right, distracted by her serving responsibilities, but Mary chose to sit at Jesus' feet. When Martha complained to Jesus that she was doing all the work, Jesus replied that Mary had chosen the ONE THING that was most important, undistracted devotion to Him.

"The Lord answered her, "Martha, my beloved Martha. Why are you upset and troubled, pulled away by all these many distractions? Mary has discovered

the one thing most important by choosing to sit at my feet. She is undistracted, and I won't take this privilege from her."" (Matthew 26:13)

To stay in this place of ministering to the Lord whilst serving and building the Kingdom takes discipline of our flesh, obedience to the Word and most of all – love, a relentless pursuit of the King, the One who loves us more than any other!

"But I discipline my body and bring it into subjection, lest, when I have preached to others, I myself should become disqualified." (I Corinthians 9:27 NKJV)

The Bible promises that we can be confident that God will complete in us the work that He started, and we have no doubt of this promise. This journey on earth will continue until He calls us home to glory!

"Being confident of this very thing, that He who has begun a good work in you will complete it until the day of Jesus Christ." (Philippians 1:6 NKJV)

The part we must play is to remain in Him, seeking His Face, abiding in Him, giving Him our perpetual 'YES!' His plans for us are far better than anything we can think or imagine and as we continue to follow His lead for our lives, knowing that as He guides, He is also our protection and our rear guard; we cannot help but finish our race well.

DO YOU KNOW HIM?

Finally, before I finish this book, I cannot end without giving you, the reader, the opportunity to meet your Creator.

I pray, as you have read about our journey, that it has testified of the goodness of God, the unconditional love of the Father, the grace and mercy of the Saviour. I pray that you have remembered times in your own journey when God has pursued you, protected you, called you to Himself.

If you haven't yet met Jesus, if you haven't encountered God the Father or felt the presence of the Holy Spirit, would you like to? He is just a prayer away.

Ask Him to reveal Himself to you, ask Him to forgive you. Maybe you have asked Christ into your life before but have walked away or became distracted with the things of the world; maybe you have become lukewarm.

If you have decided that you want to give your whole life to Jesus, I invite you to pray this prayer:

HEAVENLY FATHER,
I COME BEFORE YOU IN THIS MOMENT AND I REPENT OF ALL MY
SIN. JESUS, I BELIEVE THAT YOU DIED ON THE CROSS TO PAY THE
PRICE FOR EVERY TIME I HAVE SINNED OR FALLEN SHORT.
I BELIEVE THAT YOU ROSE FROM THE DEAD AND ARE NOW SEATED
AT THE RIGHT HAND OF THE FATHER IN HEAVEN, VICTORIOUS OVER
SIN AND DEATH.
JESUS, I GIVE MY WHOLE LIFE TO YOU, I CONFESS YOU AS MY LORD
AND SAVIOUR.
HOLY SPIRIT, FILL ME WITH YOUR PRESENCE. TEACH ME, LEAD ME,
GUIDE ME INTO ALL TRUTH.
HELP ME TO FOLLOW YOU ALL THE DAYS OF MY LIFE.
IN JESUS MIGHTY AND PRECIOUS NAME,
AMEN

If you prayed this prayer for the first time, or if you are recommitting your life to the Lord, I would love to hear from you! Please send me an email and let me know so I can celebrate with you.

My email address is tabby72@gmail.com